No Cloak, No Dagger

ALLIED SPYCRAFT IN OCCUPIED FRANCE

Benjamin Cowburn

Foreword by Sebastian Faulks
Introduction by M.R.D. Foot

Frontline Books, London

No Cloak, No Dagger
This paperback edition published in 2014 by
Frontline Books
an imprint of
Pen & Sword Books Ltd,
47 Church Street, Barnsley,
S. Yorkshire, S70 2AS
www.frontline-books.com

This edition © Pen & Sword Books Ltd, 2014
Foreword © Sebastian Faulks, 2014
Introduction © M.R.D. Foot, 2014

The right of Benjamin Cowburn to be identified as the author of
this work has been asserted by him in accordance with the
Copyright, Designs and Patents Act 1988.

ISBN: 978-1-84832-776-4

Publishing History
No Cloak, No Dagger was first published in 1960 by the Adventure Club,
Brown, Watson and Jarrolds, London. A new edition was published in 2009 by
Frontline Books, an imprint of Pen & Sword Books Ltd. The publishers would
like to gratefully acknowledge the assistance of Roderick Suddaby and Roderick
Bailey at London's Imperial War Museum in the reissue of this edition.

CIP data records for this title are available from the British Library

For more information on our books, please visit
www.frontline-books.com, email info@frontline-books.com
or write to us at the above address.

Printed and bound by
CPI Group (UK) Ltd, Croydon, CR0 4YY

Contents

Foreword

Discovering exactly what happened in the past is never easy. History, as we know, is written by those who end up with the power to do so, and such people seldom care – or even know – what it felt like to the individual. Then there is the problem of politics – the peculiar human prejudice that can't accommodate the subtleties of truth, and to which even the most honourable historians are susceptible.

The story of the Special Operations Executive in World War Two has some extra problems all of its own. SOE had an uneasy relationship with Britain's 'official' Secret Intelligence Service, SIS or MI6. The Roundheads of SIS looked down on the Cavalier saboteurs of SOE, whose loud explosions, they believed, compromised their own careful planning. But after the war, SOE became to some extent infected by the institutional furtiveness of SIS and by its sometimes undemocratic attitude to national security. Not everything that subsequently emerged with an SOE imprimatur was as straight as it looked. And as if this were not bad enough, it must also be admitted that many SOE agents were themselves untrustworthy or vainglorious; not even their personal recollections are quite reliable.

It is against this murky background that Benjamin Cowburn's *No Cloak, No Dagger*, first published in 1960, still shines bright and true. Here is the terse, anti-heroic tone of factual recall; this, you feel, is what it was like. From the first sentence, as he is helped into a Whitley bomber for his first drop, to the last, which remembers those who did not return, Cowburn gives the distinct flavour of occupied France in those desperate early years. The reader has the thrilling sensation that he has been simply and truthfully taken back in time.

No one could invent the smell of the inside of a military aircraft without having been there as often as Cowburn was; no one would have noticed the nose-down flying attitude of a Whitley unless he'd been lying on the fuselage floor. Few other SOE memoirists would have contented themselves with the laconic: 'During the next few days I travelled about the south by train to obtain certain information.'

It is not only the details that are impressive. Cowburn's political judgments – of Pétain, Laval and Darlan, of the effects of Mers el Kébir and Dakar – are simple but sure-footed. The political story has been enlarged by later historians, but Cowburn's rapid field assessment has not essentially been superseded. He is a realist in a complicated situation. If he is a fraction more indulgent towards the behaviour of the occupied French than later writers have been, I think this is understandable on two grounds. First, Benjamin Cowburn knew Resistance fighters not just in 1943, when young Frenchmen joined up in their thousands to avoid being shipped off to work in German factories, but in the hard early days when they were very few in number and almost all French public opinion was against them. Cowburn worked closely with these men, and I for one trust his judgment of them. The other reason is that without the efforts of these 1941–2 volunteers, native Resistance and SOE alike, there would have been no soul of France worth saving. Keeping the faith sometimes means having to turn a blind eye or mute your criticism; but their belief, their tactics and their courage were finally vindicated. France survived, if not with her honour intact then at least with a slender unbroken connection to the past that General de Gaulle and others could claim represented the continuing, the essential *patrie*.

I came across *No Cloak, No Dagger* in 1995 when writing a novel called *Charlotte Gray*, and reading it again now fourteen years later I find myself wanting to mark down certain passages that I might want to incorporate as background colour. The silence of the grands boulevards in Paris with no traffic roar; the importance of placing explosive material flush against the machinery it is intended to destroy . . . And then the detail that in 1995 made me feel that perhaps I was on to a good thing (and you always need such encouragements in the early stages of a venture): Cowburn's revelation that the SOE codename for the moon was Charlotte.

Cowburn writes in a plain vernacular, but his prose can rise to the occasion. Take the moonlit chapter on the Munitions Drop, for instance; or the description of his crossing the demarcation line in a hollow beneath the tender of a locomotive; or the paean to the small Lysander plane – the Spitfire of the SOE, to whom it became a much-loved symbol of their slightly ramshackle efforts . . . At all these moments, Benjamin Cowburn's writing, without losing its factual edge, is flexible enough to convey something more than adventure: something, however much he might have resisted the word, heroic.

Cowburn is at pains to downplay the bravery required by himself and his French and SOE friends to keep the light of France burning. That is his privilege, and we surely can allow him his modesty; we can grant to him and his one-eyed major friend, desperate to bag another four Boche for his century, their reluctance even from beyond the grave to 'shoot a line'. In return, perhaps, they wouldn't mind so much if at this remove we still offer our respect and admiration for what they did.

No Cloak, No Dagger epitomises so much of what was best in the early years of the British war effort, not just in SOE but in what Cowburn calls the Poor Bloody Infantry and the RAF as well. If there is a better SOE memoir, I hope someone will tell me its name.

Sebastian Faulks, 2009

Introduction

There are plenty of weak books about SOE, the special operations executive of which the task was to spread mayhem in Axis-occupied countries during the world war of 1939–45. This is one of the strong ones: a brief, telling account of what being a special agent on duty actually felt like at the time. Few other books are half as vivid; few other authors had quite so many sorties into danger, or quite so much luck in escaping it.

Ben Cowburn was a Lancashire-born oil engineer, in his early thirties when the war against Hitler began, who had been brought up in France and – rarely enough for an Englishman – spoke good unaccented French. He was short, stockily built, with straight sandy hair and a toothbrush moustache, quite unexciting in his looks. His command of French drew him to SOE's attention; he was posted away from his infantry unit to these special duties, passed the usual paramilitary training courses and a parachute course, and dropped into France as early as the night of 6/7 September 1941. Already an army captain, he was of course dressed in plain clothes of French appearance, even if made in Soho, and fortified with a mass of false papers, including a certificate of demobilisation from the French army in which he had notionally fought in the summer catastrophe of 1940. Such papers were forged for SOE at its Station XIV at Briggens Hotel near Harlow, by the cream of the Polish and British forgery professions who happened to be out of prison when approached; they were usually undetectable as forgeries.

For his first few days back in France, he found it hard to remember that his false identity was not written on his face but soon got used to behaving as if he still belonged there, and got on with his work. He had a task of strategic importance, to inspect as many French oil refineries as he could reach and report on how they could be sabotaged. Brooks Richards has a good story, in his fine *Secret Flotillas*, of Cowburn's sabotage of a refinery he had built with his own hands; but the agent himself confessed that he had not been able to tackle any of his targets, the guards were too stiff.

He also found out a great deal about conditions of life in wartime France, and found his own way of crossing the demarcation line between the occupied and non-occupied zones: hidden underneath the body of a large railway locomotive that ran between Bordeaux and Montauban, in a cavity into and out of which he was helped by friendly railwaymen – who asked no questions and accepted no payment.

He soon got swept up into the orbit of Pierre de Vomécourt, alias Lucas, his section's first important agent in France, a Lorrainer baron educated in England who did wonders to get SOE's independent French section on to its working feet. This took him back to Paris, which looked more beautiful than ever when deprived of its plinth of motorcars. Unhappily Lucas was embrangled with a sergeant in the Abwehr, the German armed forces' security service, called Hugo Bleicher, who pretended to be a colonel in the German army of anti-Nazi leanings. ('I did not think he could be a colonel,' Cowburn said, 'he wore such cheap shoes'.) Madame Carré who was Lucas's link with a wireless operator turned out to be a double agent, working for the Abwehr; hideous complications ensued, which led Cowburn to make an escape on foot over the Pyrenees into Spain.

He got safely back to England, and was soon despatched on a second mission, parachuting into the Limousin on 1/2 June 1942. He again made touch with a rich farmer called Chantraine, who had received him on his first drop and, like so many wealthy peasants, supported the communist party as least likely to take away his land. He was able to organize a little sabotage round Châteauroux, but without a wireless operator of his own could not get much going; he returned, this time by Lysander light aircraft, in October. He gives a lively account of exactly how the Lysander trip was run.

His third mission was more productive. Again he went in by parachute, this time south of Blois on 11 April 1943, with John

Barrett (called Honoré) as his wireless man. They set up a circuit, codenamed Tinker, round Troyes, and brought off a splendid sabotage coup, putting a dozen railway engines out of action in a single night. Preparing this, Cowburn made one mistake: he lectured his whole team of saboteurs in a schoolroom, showing on a blackboard exactly what they were going to do, and forgot to wipe the blackboard clean. Luck was with him; the headmaster's wife (whose husband was on the team) saw it before school opened, and made all safe. Unaccountably, this coup was left out of Tony Brooks's summary made at the end of the war of all the circuit's best demolitions.

The Germans were much put out by this coup, and Cowburn got out by Lysander in September, leaving the circuit in charge of his friend Pierre Mulsant a local timber merchant, who later came out by air also, bringing Barrett with him. These last two went back to France in March 1944 to set up a new sabotage circuit in the Seine-et-Marne, just south-east of Paris, but got arrested during the midsummer turmoil of 1944. Cowburn made a fourth sortie by parachute in July to try to rescue them, but too late; they were murdered that autumn in Buchenwald.

Cowburn describes how mercilessly mean town life was in Pétain's two-fifths of France, that was unoccupied by the German army until November 1942. Shops were still open, but had hardly anything worth buying to sell. Food was short to the verge of famine, except on the black market, in which villains were lining their own pockets. Coffee had vanished, replaced by an odious dark brown liquid that almost made him (and me) vomit, composed from acorns. Croissants and baguettes had vanished too, replaced by barely eatable dark bread. There were no fewer than fifteen separate police forces, competing with each other to enforce a myriad of new rules (every bicycle, for example, had to have its own number-plate). Even in occupied France, everybody equipped himself with a little box in which to store cigarette-ends, later to be repacked into further cigarettes, as well as another to hold such little sugar as was to be found on the ration – it was no longer served in cafés.

He knew, only too well, the risks he himself ran, and did what he could to minimise the risks run by his helpers; but acknowledges, over and over again, that they ran much worse risks even than he did. As well as all Vichy's police forces, they had to contend in the occupied zone both with the Abwehr and with the deadlier Gestapo, the secret state police. He knew that on his first mission he must have been seen by several Abwehr agents, one at least of whom had probably photographed him, and that the Gestapo had at least heard of him, if they had not yet bothered to investigate him. He thought that, given luck as well as courage, he could steer clear of both these bodies; but his French helpers, however brave, were much less likely to be lucky, because they were tied down by businesses, houses, wives, sometimes children – all of them liable to seizure if anything went wrong. It was an offence even to tune in to the BBC; many of his helpers went a great deal farther than that. Luckily for all the circuits he headed, he was an extra prudent agent; terrors enough remained.

His four sorties into France were exceptional – I only know of one agent who did more, Victor Gerson who was with him on his first operational jump, but then went off on a separate mission to organize the secret and effective 'Vic' escape line, and re-entered France secretly six more times. That wayward stream the fount of honour played rather oddly on Cowburn: for all his gallantry and his efficiency, he was fobbed off with a military cross, while over a score of his fellow circuit organizers – some of them not half his worth – were appointed to the distinguished service order. He was probably too outspoken to be cosseted with fine gongs. Here is his book, at any rate, reprinted after nearly fifty years, to explain to us what he and the secret life he led were really like. He returned to Paris after the war, and married a former secretary to Georges Bidault, a leading figure in the Fourth Republic. He died early in 1994. Both Great Britain and France owe him a great debt.

M.R.D. Foot, 2009

Preface

This is not a complete account of my war experiences, but simply an attempt to describe the impressions of a British officer engaged on a special mission in France during the German occupation. To this end I have selected a number of episodes, scenes and details—all authentic—which I consider typical.

Those of us who had the privilege of living with the French during their ordeal are able to understand their inner feelings, their distrust of politicians who led them to disaster and their contempt for bureaucracy, which was, in their minds, associated with the application of restrictions imposed by the enemy.

The calamity of occupation brings out the worst and the best. Like my brother-agents, I saw both. The worst was shameful. The best was fine, as fine as could be found anywhere.

1. Fly R.A.F. to the Continent

ON A clear windless evening in early September 1941 we were being helped into a Whitley bomber on an aerodrome about sixty miles north of London. We certainly needed assistance; our flying-suits, parachute harnesses and packs had turned us into clumsy human sausages.

In those days, moreover, separate luggage-parachutes were not yet provided and we could take only such personal effects as could be stuffed into our flying-suits. This made us even clumsier. My pyjamas, in particular, made a rather ludicrous bulge. In fact, I had been allowed to retain them only after an argument in the dressing-hut with a very tall and superior Guards officer (staff, of course) who could not see that the likes of us should need pyjamas. Only the wireless-transmitter which one of my fellow-passengers was taking had its own special packing. It hung in a foam-rubber-lined bag from the roof of the fuselage directly above the exit-hole in the floor. It was to be attached by strops to its owner's rigging, so that both George (all wireless-operators were known as 'George' in those days) and his transmitter would go down together under the same parachute.

There were six of us in this single operation. Each had a different destination, but due, I believe, to a shortage of aircraft and reception facilities, we were to jump together near Châteauroux and then proceed separately to our various destinations in France.

We had been told that this was not to be a 'blind' drop, but that a reception committee would show lights on the ground to guide the aircraft to the spot chosen for the drop, and that they would also help us on arrival.

At the door we took leave of our guardian angel, Thomas Cadett (poor Thomas! he had had to be patient as an angel at times with our crowd!), and we clambered along inside the fuselage to the various positions we were to occupy for the flight. The floor was formed by the top of the long low bomb-bay and we lay on it with our heads and shoulders propped against the sides of the long corridor-like hull.

The air was filled with that odour peculiar to military aircraft —a light, oily, tinny smell. All was quiet outside as the door was closed and the twilight shut out. After a short pause the engines started and we began to move. We felt the acceleration and bumping of the take-off and soon had settled down to cruising speed.

Inside the fuselage with us were the R.A.F. sergeants who were to act as dispatchers. They were helpers, stewards and advisers to us during these operations. They brought refreshments and gave us information. In particular, it was the dispatcher's job to attach the automatic-opening strop, known as the static line, to your parachute. The principle is that, as operational parachutists are dropped, for accuracy, from too low an altitude to have time to open the canopy themselves, the bag containing the parachute is tethered by means of this strop to a point inside the fuselage. As the man drops away and the strop is pulled taut, it holds back the bag, thus liberating the canopy a short distance below the plane. Whenever the dispatcher made the attachment, he always showed you the connection, so you could feel sure your 'chute would open.

The curious nose-down flying attitude of the Whitley was quite obvious from inside. Though I was lying on the floor I could see that the fuselage was sloping upwards towards the tail and asked the dispatcher if we were going down. He said, no, we were even climbing slowly.

There were no windows and we were reclining on the floor, almost unable to move in the dimness. At the forward end was the partition which hid from our view the nose section containing the controls and flying crew. Right at the stern was the rear-gunner in his revolving turret. The exit-hole was a short distance aft of the forward partition and was covered by boards.

George IX, the owner of the transmitter, lay forward of the hole, and I just aft of it, with the four other 'bodies' further along the fuselage. The order of exit was to be: first George and his wireless-set, then myself, then one more man. The aircraft was then to circle and drop the last three during a second run over the target, as it was felt that six men in a single row (or stick) would be dispersed over too great an area. Running these arrangements over in our minds, we settled down for the three-hour journey.

The uneasiness I was feeling was quite different from the anxiety of the practice jumps. I was no longer worried about banging my face on the opposite edge of the hole . . . or getting hurt while landing. This time there was no worrying about the mechanics of the jump itself, as there was a chance of a great deal more bother after reaching the ground. Also, there was the feeling of being cut off from normal surroundings and of entering a new world.

As we approached the Channel the meagre lighting was switched off and we were in the dark. When the dispatchers moved about amidst the tangle of legs and webbing straps they used hand torches, which made the hanging radio-bag look rather sinister as it swung gently to and fro over the cover of the exit-hole.

When we were over the Channel we were told that if we heard firing it would probably be the rear-gunner testing his guns and not necessarily a scrap with a Messerschmitt. One of the principles of the Royal Air Force was that every bit of equipment should function perfectly. The least sign of a defect in the operation of any component would mean a return home. It was only on this condition that they would ask men to fly over enemy territory, and that was probably why I never had any fear of my parachute failing to open.

So we droned on through the night. I was surprised to find

myself dozing. We all seemed to have no difficulty in dropping off to sleep as we were advised to do by the dispatcher with the assurance that he would see we did not 'miss our station'. In fact he had to awaken me from a nap to say we were passing over Tours and that we should soon reach the target. He raised the two halves of the exit-hole cover and George and I could then look down and see the moonlit ground passing below. The pale light which came up was supplemented by a small electric lamp. We were soon over the then unoccupied part of France, and there were a few lights in the streets of the towns. It was Saturday night and about the time when people were going home from the cinemas.

There was a certain amount of bustle inside the aircraft as we were made ready. We were losing height and then came the news that the ground-signals had been spotted. George and I moved right up to the opposite edges of the hole with the radio-bag swaying between us. A little red light appeared on the wall. George swung his feet down into the hole and remained poised on the edge by his hands. The dispatcher raised his arm, the engine note changed, and the floor heaved up and down as the captain levelled out at the altitude of 500 feet prescribed for dropping. The red light changed to green, down came the dispatcher's arm, and George and his radio-bag vanished with a crash, leaving nothing but the strop of the static line hanging down through the hole.

As I in turn swung my legs out over space, I could not help thinking that it was rather like a conjuring trick. I pushed with the palms of my hands on the edge and suddenly there was another conjuring trick as the whole aeroplane vanished and I was blasted head over heels by a torrent of wind. The canopy opened and first held me flat on my face in the air looking down at the ground. Then I began to swing to and fro like a great pendulum through ever-decreasing arcs until I was floating straight down. My stomach, which seemed to have been left behind in the plane, resumed its normal place. I hit the ground with a crack sooner than I expected. I picked myself up and was faintly surprised to find I was quite unhurt. The drop had seemed unusually short, and I later learned that we had been released from only 300 feet.

As I struck the disc which loosened the harness from the box on my chest, a man ran up to me, seized my hand and warmly welcomed me to the soil of France with the words: '*Tout va bien, camarade? Tu n'es pas blessé? Tu viendras chez moi à la ferme, tu pourras te réchauffer et manger.*'

As I returned his greeting, I thought that, after all, parachuting was a far better way of entering an occupied country than a long sea voyage.

I have described this journey at some length as dropping operations whether of agents or supplies played a major part in all our activities.

Moreover, although I have since made a considerable number of air journeys, the flight of an aeroplane still maintains its fascination for me, but I do, of course, prefer comfortable airliners which one is not required to leave through holes in the floor.

When the aircraft had finished its second run and flown away into the night, we were nine on the ground, the six 'bodies' and the three members of the reception committee. There was a bit of a fuss as one of the 'bodies' had dropped into a nearby pond and had to be fished out dripping wet. However, our 'chutes were soon collected and we made our way, filing along hedges, past barking dogs, to the farmhouse belonging to the man who had greeted me.

We heard a train in the distance and a motor-car on a nearby road. At the time there was little information in England on the exact conditions which prevailed on the Continent, and I wondered how many cars were still running.

In the kitchen of the farmhouse our host began to make a colossal omelette on the stove, the two other members of the reception committee proceeded to give us the latest information, and our sopping-wet friend undressed and spent the rest of the night drying 1000-franc banknotes at the fire. Our parachutes and flying-suits had disappeared into a hayloft.

We learned that we had arrived during the night preceding

the opening of the hunting season and that there would be a number of people about the fields and woods during the early hours of the morning. Thus we heard that hunting-guns and a few cartridges were allowed in the unoccupied zone. There was no curfew as in the occupied zone. The Vichy police were very active, and in the opinion of our hosts there was a chance of being arrested, but, of course, the consequences would not be the same as in the occupied zone.

As to food and other ration coupons—tobacco had just been drastically rationed. . . . Train services were not too bad. Clandestine passages over the demarcation line to the occupied zone were possible, but not easy, and official passes had better be left alone by people like us.

Some of us made a few arrangements for contacting each other should it be necessary, and, towards dawn, after thanking our host, we left to go our different ways.

I will now introduce these eight men, and state what eventually became of them, although we may meet some of them again in this story before their fates overtook them.

Parachutists

GEORGE IX: radio-operator, was caught in the occupied zone about ten weeks later and shot.

DENIS: was caught in the occupied zone about eight months later and deported to Germany, but was liberated at the end of the war.

RENE: was able to carry on all through the war and escape detection.

TROTTOBAS: was caught about six weeks later in the unoccupied zone, but subsequently escaped and returned to do a grand job in the occupied zone. He was killed in a gun-battle with the Gestapo (Captain Michel).

MARCEL: was caught about a month later in the unoccupied zone, but subsequently escaped.

MYSELF: was very lucky.

Reception Committee

GEORGE I: this was George Noble, radio-operator. He had been the *first* member of our particular organization to be dropped and to establish secret radio communication with home. At the time of our arrival he was our only means of sending messages. He was caught about a month later in the unoccupied zone, but subsequently escaped.

MAX: this was M. Max Hymans, a French Member of Parliament, who was helping George I. He had to go into hiding about a month later to avoid capture and subsequently reached England. He now holds a very important and well-deserved position in France.

OCTAVE: this was a rich farmer named Chantraine who was Mayor of Tendu. It was at his farm we were entertained. He worked splendidly until near the end of the occupation. He was finally caught and put to death.

I have made the above list only in order to give an idea of the casualty rate among the early participants in secret warfare.

2. First impressions

TROTT and I decided to walk together to the nearest town, Argenton-sur-Creuse, and part at the railway station. I was to travel south to attend to some business there and later cross the demarcation line and go to Paris.

From the farmhouse we went along a cart-track and lane, then decided to wait until daybreak under a hedge before taking to the main road. When it grew lighter we resumed our walk. We had about ten miles to go and we began to enjoy the exercise and the scenery. At a small hamlet by the road we saw two gendarmes alight from their bicycles. They took not the slightest notice of us, but went into a tiny café. We realized that it would take us a few hours to get used to the idea that what we knew about ourselves was not written on our faces. This may seem childish, but it should be recalled that dropping into the middle of another country was quite a novelty at the time and no one knew just what to expect. Later on it became much more of a routine and conditions inside France came to be well known to the headquarters in London.

We had thought that as there were very few motor-cars running we would meet a number of pedestrians along the road, but this was not the case. Most of the few people we saw in the early hours were on bicycles. As we were to find out, the bicycle was the queen of the road and a man riding one at any hour was far less conspicuous than a pedestrian, as he made little noise and remained in sight for a much shorter time. Also, clothing and parcels of weird and wonderful shape seemed quite fitting on a bicycle. A further advantage was that, if questioned, a cyclist could claim to have ridden from any spot, however distant, whereas it would seem less natural if a fairly well-dressed man claimed to have been walking or even hitch-hiking for twenty or thirty miles.

However, the authorities had apparently not guessed what the low-flying plane had been doing the night before, and there was no net around the area from which it had turned back. Besides, in order to 'cover' this kind of operation, propaganda leaflets were generally dropped on neighbouring towns.

After walking for about three hours we reached the pretty little town of Argenton-sur-Creuse. It was a pleasant Sunday morning and most of the people were in the streets. They appeared to be not too badly dressed, except that a number of them clattered along on wooden-soled shoes, but in a small country town this did not seem out of place.

The displays in the shops were mostly rubbish. (How shops could stay open with only such trash to sell was a perpetual source of wonder throughout the occupation.) Nevertheless, coupons or permits were required for almost everything. We had ersatz 'coffee' (a horrible bitter brew) sweetened with saccharine pellets. In every shop-window and on the wall in every café was a photograph of Le Maréchal with one of his sayings. At lunch-time, we went to an hotel to find out how the fake food-ration cards which had been supplied in London would work. The waiter clipped some of the coupons and we ate a modest meal. The bread was dreadful (50 grams per 'ticket').

A little simple arithmetic soon showed that in practice a human being could not subsist on the quantities awarded by the monthly ration cards and it therefore became obvious that we should soon discover the black market. However, we had enough coupons to exist 'legally' for the time being.

We had decided to be very cautious and not to display our ignorance of prevailing conditions by asking for normally unobtainable things, but we did make one or two slips, such as trying to buy cigarettes without a tobacco card. However, the way in which our requests were received showed that we were

B

merely suspected of attempting to get something 'black market', which was quite a normal thing to do, and the refusal was generally courteous.

When we went to the station to catch the afternoon train, I again experienced faint surprise that the booking-office clerk should sell us tickets without taking any notice, and resolved to get rid of the feeling that I was a 'being from outer space' as quickly as possible.

Trott was getting out at an earlier station than I, so we said goodbye on the platform and got into different carriages. As the train ran swiftly southwards through the French countryside, I felt that I had really entered my new life.

I alighted in the evening at Toulouse, where I intended to spend the night.

As I left the station of this large city I began to see the shabbiness and meanness which characterized the 'New Order'. 'New Order' was the official title which Marshal Pétain had bestowed on France's way of life with the German noose around her neck.

The dilapidated horse-carriages at the former taxi-stands, the cyclists towing light two-wheeled passenger-trailers, conveyed a painful impression of deterioration. There were trams but only a few motor-cars. I went for a quick look at the shops and was fortunate enough to find a reasonably presentable fibre suitcase. Into this I put my rolled parcel containing my few personal belongings and entered an hotel opposite the station. I filled up the registration card under my new name and went up to my room.

I had no qualms about going to an hotel for a night. My luggage was innocent enough. I had 25,000 francs, which was not a very large amount, and also a little pack of lies to go with it.

In my shabby room there was a notice warning that shoes left outside the door for cleaning were frequently stolen and that the management could therefore not be held responsible for them.

I went out to explore the town. Most of the few cars and motor-lorries were running by means of *gazogènes* or charcoal-gas generators, which supplied gas fuel to the engine instead of petrol.

I was later to learn all about them, and if ever I were asked to propose a test of motoring 'know-how' I would suggest trying to start one of these contraptions on a cold morning, without the trick of using a pint of carefully hoarded petrol before switching over to the gas.

The town was dull and the people looked dispirited. I became aware of another sign of the times besides the omnipresent photographs of Marshal Pétain—the many notices giving directions for sending parcels to prisoners of war. Well over a million Frenchmen of military age were prisoners in Germany. This meant that seven or eight million wives, relatives and friends must be hanging on by their heart-strings, going without some of their meagre supplies in order to send food and clothing to Germany and living for the arrival of the letters saying their men were well. It must have been the same anxiety which British dependants of fighting men were feeling, but with the added thought that it had all been in vain. I felt I was looking at an open wound.

During the next few days I travelled about the south by train to obtain certain information. There were fewer trains than in peace-time, but they were punctual and clean. I often spotted the keen eyes of obvious plain-clothes policemen on watch at the station barriers, where luggage would frequently be searched, not only for weapons, but also for food.

In the unoccupied zone everything was 'national'—the Marshal was trying to stir up a feeling of officialized patriotism. It was, of course, to be an emasculated patriotism in which the French were *not* to dream of booting the Germans clean out of the country as a first objective. Oh, no! France was being punished for soft living—perhaps the punishment *had* exceeded their deserts—but defeat must be accepted as an institution and the French were to be taught to find a new glory in repentance. This call to prance on the end of a leash attracted a multitude of little cads and job-hunters who obtained employment in all manner of 'national' agencies—anything from controlling food supplies to diffusing propaganda or acting as police informers. Such 'work' entitled them to some sort of a special card which made them feel privileged and in a position to push their fellow-countrymen around.

The tricolour emblem appeared everywhere. Officially the citizen got all he was entitled to by kind permission of the police-state. All sorts of inferior goods were palmed off on to him wrapped up in the flag. Never have the words 'Patrie—Honneur—Courage' appeared so frequently in official speeches and newspaper articles.

I, of course, read the newspapers with their sorry toadying blurbs and wondered what effect this would have on the average Frenchman.

In the streets one would frequently see platoons of children dressed in glorified Boy Scout uniforms straggling along behind a flag, singing songs, the verses of which ended in a shortly barked syllable in imitation of the German marching songs.

In all the towns were the same bicycle-trailers with their human power unit, the gazogène motor-vehicles and the horse-drawn carriages.

In the suburban areas and in the country Queen Bicycle held the road.

The people one met on the trains were careful not to express their feelings about the situation, but their very reticence encouraged me to believe I would soon find a lot under the surface.

I cautiously called on some friends I had known before the war. They were an average young French couple with a little boy. They gave me a warm welcome, shared such food as they had with me and we had a long conversation. When they had got over the wonder of my arriving out of the blue they asked me about England. I told them that the British were full of beans and would in due course beat the Germans. I told them of the Battle of Britain, but they, like a lot of French people, had not realized the importance of this nor what a thrashing the Luftwaffe had received. They had not, on the other hand, believed the stories about London being completely destroyed.

They did not know what to think of General de Gaulle. They had listened to the Free French broadcasts from London but did not know whether to believe them or not. They asked whether the British were the allies of the dreaded Russian Communists. I replied that we were both fighting the same enemy, but they need have no fear that we would allow the Communists to govern France. Well, there I was, a living proof that the sons of 'perfidious Albion' could wander about without the permission of either Hitler or Pétain!

They described the confusion in the mind of the average Frenchman. What it amounted to was this: in 1940 the Army had collapsed, the Germans were speeding across the north of France, taking the French Forces piecemeal and driving the British into the sea. Large sections of the population were fleeing along the congested roads in the nightmare exodus. The existing government had panicked and thrust the supreme command into the hands of the aged Marshal Pétain who had just been recalled from retirement. I believe he really did think he could negotiate a truce in the old nineteenth-century style. He little realized, however, that this was the age of total war, unconditional surrender and the enslavement of conquered countries.

His representatives met Hitler, a demarcation line was drawn on the map, the German columns which were advancing southwards towards Marseilles withdrew and the refugees began to make their way back home.

So the residents of one-third of France found themselves out of the war and relieved of the presence of the enemy. Those troops who had managed to reach the south in the rout were demobilized on the spot. (According to my papers I was one of these!)

The politicians who had been in power up to the time of the collapse had vanished with all their false prophecies, as had the generals who used to make such glowing reports on the perfect fitness and organization of the Army, together with the official morale-boosters with their stories that German soldiers were only too eager to desert, German shells failed to explode, German motor-lorries invariably broke down and German aircraft were badly designed flying coffins.

Marshal Pétain appealed to the people as a glorious old general who was swallowing the bitter pill of a defeat for which he was not responsible and ministering to them in their misery at the risk of losing his own reputation. He could not be suspected of toadying to the Germans and would be respected by Hitler. He had given them a watchword, '*Travail—Famille—Patrie*', telling them that they must not revolt, as that would rock the leaky boat and they must withdraw into a day-to-day existence however drab and be glad they still had that. Unoccupied France must keep herself to herself. No arguments must divide the people. The only opinions allowed expression were those which flattered the present government.

The sinister, dirty-looking face of Laval appeared beside the Marshal but was thought to be held in check. The vain, England-hating Admiral Darlan was acting as the Marshal's deputy, but it was considered that he also was kept in his place.

As far as England was concerned, there were mixed feelings. The memory of the tragedy at Mers-el-Kébir was still strong and had been exploited to the hilt by the enemy's propaganda service.

Certainly they understood that the British Government could not, in such critical circumstances, tolerate the presence of a powerful naval squadron which might pass, even indirectly, under German control, but the death-roll had been heavy.

The ridiculous fiasco at Dakar had not enhanced our reputation either. Lastly, the clash in Syria had just ended, but we had acted more firmly there. I had already heard several repatriated French N.C.O.s talking about this in railway trains. They bore no grudge and gave the impression that the British had been rather sporting about it. One sergeant had told how, after he was neatly captured, a British N.C.O. had driven him back to base on the pillion of a motor-cycle!

The Germans had thrown us out of Greece and were going great guns in Russia.

The record up to date was therefore not very brilliant. Still, most Frenchmen refused to believe in a German victory. They lived in the hope that England would not be beaten, that somehow she would win the final battle, particularly since the fighting on the Russian front would give her a breathing spell. Then, of course, there was the overriding fact that the Nazis had failed to land in England.

Thus I obtained my first impressions of the 'free' zone with its atmosphere of German threat, but I was keen to enter the occupied zone and sample the other atmosphere—that of German presence.

3. First signs of trouble

BEFORE crossing the demarcation line on my way to Paris, I returned to Châteauroux to see George I, who was to give me the address of George IX, my flight companion and future wireless-operator. The latter had set off for Paris at once and we had agreed that, as soon as he was settled there, he would send a message to George I giving directions for contacting him. This message was to be sent by courier or, if that proved impracticable, by wireless to H.Q., who would relay it to George I.

To contact George I, I went to the address of a 'letter-drop' he had given me, but the man there was jittery and said he had broken off connections as he felt sure he was being watched. In spite of this negative beginning, I did eventually manage to find George I, but he had as yet no news of George IX, except that he knew he had succeeded in crossing the demarcation line. We arranged another meeting for a week later in the restaurant where he took his meals.

I went south for another exploratory journey in the meantime.

When I returned to Châteauroux things were really bad, and I will state briefly what occurred, as this kind of situation was to become commonplace.

As I was leaving the train in Châteauroux station, I met, quite by chance, Marcel, one of my fellow-passengers from England. He also was looking for George I. I suggested that the simplest thing would be for us to meet George at dinner, but Marcel said no, he wanted to see him as soon as possible. He was going to put a letter in one of George's 'letter-drops' and arrange an appointment in a café late that afternoon. He wrote out his note and, as I had nothing better to do, I walked with him to a house behind the town barracks. (It was not the same 'letter-drop' I had tried a few days before.) There was a letter-box flap in the door, into which Marcel dropped his note. We then separated and went to book rooms in different hotels.

I went to the restaurant at dinner-time, but neither George nor Marcel came. I was quite surprised, as one of the two, at least, should have appeared. Following our usual procedure, I returned to lunch at the same place the next day, but again found neither.

As I had thought I would meet George I on the first evening, I had booked a room for one night only. I asked to be allowed to stay on, but that hotel was full and I had to move to another.

I returned to the restaurant that evening, hoping to find George at last. There was still no sign of him, but seated at a table I saw two men, one of whom I recognized as a brother officer I had met in one of our special training schools. This happy coincidence was to be the first of my many lucky breaks. We left the restaurant together and I was introduced to the second man, Lucas, who had been dropped several months before. In fact he had followed close behind George I and was the very first member of our organization to have entered Occupied France. He was our agent in Paris.

My training companion, whom I shall call Gerald, had just arrived by sea on the south coast. They had both, for different purposes, been looking for George I, and gave me the news. George I was 'blown' and so was Max. The Châteauroux organization, including the 'letter-drop' people, had been arrested. Just where George himself was, and whether he was still at liberty, was not clear. They knew nothing of Marcel. They had, moreover, taken serious risks in order to get this information.

However, Lucas had one item of good news. It was precisely he who had received in Paris the very man I wanted to find, our second radio-operator, my dropping companion, George IX. He was able to tell me how to contact him and, as he was going back to Paris, we made an appointment to meet there a few days later.

Lucas was well established in Paris. He was a Frenchman and had been able to slip back into his normal life without anyone suspecting that during his absence after the collapse of France he had spent several months in England. He had an *Ausweiss*, or official pass, to cross the line, whereas I had to find a secret way.

I returned to my new hotel and was having a drink in the bar and meditating on the frailty of things in general and of secret agents' arrangements in particular when the manageress came and said there were two gentlemen outside on the pavement who would like to speak to me. I thought they must be my two friends who had forgotten to tell me something, and sauntered out.

They were, however, two strangers. One of them said: 'We are the police!' Bang! I was busy trying to think how to acknowledge this charming greeting when the same man asked: 'Have you anything in your room?'

—Well, of course, I have my luggage, but what do you want of me, anyway?

—What is there in your luggage?

—Oh, well, would you not like to see for yourself?

—Certainly.

—Then come on up.

They followed me into the hall, past people who were all watching out of the corners of their eyes, and up the stairs. As I went on ahead of them along the corridor, I was thinking: 'Damn it! I really did not last very long, did I?'

Inside my room they looked around, and I looked at them. They were young and wiry looking. They asked for my papers, which I produced, and began asking questions. 'What was I doing here? What did I do for a living?' I began dealing out my pack of lies and then stopped with an embarrassed air. . . . 'Pardon me, gentlemen, but, you know . . . one hears stories . . . only yesterday in the papers . . . hem . . . there was a case of bogus policemen . . . robbing people . . . no offence meant . . . but the article *did* say police-inspectors would produce their cards of request . . . so . . . well?'

The two men said, 'Why, of course!' their hands flew to their pockets and they each whipped out an important-looking identity card with a photograph and tricolour bands across the corner. I deprecatingly waved them aside, saying: 'Oh! that's quite all right! . . . I hope you didn't mind?'

—No! not at all.

—You see, I cannot imagine whatever the police would want with me.

—Oh, this is just a simple check-up.

This request to see their papers had apparently struck them as unusual for a man who had something on his mind, and they turned away from me and began looking under the bed and inside the wardrobe.

I was thinking fast. There were three possibilities. The first was, of course, that their visit was connected with the George affair—perhaps my friends and I had been spotted and followed. It was quite possible we were all caught in the net.

The second was that as I had changed hotels, my name had turned up twice running in the police register and this might have singled me out for attention.

The third was that some police spy had picked me out on suspicion that I might be a 'wanted' man.

I discounted the 'routine check-up', as no one else in the hotel was challenged.

Now it was vital that I should not be taken to the police-station, as my identity papers were entirely bogus. A phone call or telegram to the town given as the place of issue would have revealed I was a 'phoney'. The two inspectors were not examining my underclothing or toilet accessories in any great detail and it occurred to me they were looking for a bulkier object. Was it George's wireless-transmitter they were after?

Suddenly one of them strode to the night-table, on which lay a leather case. 'You have a camera!' He opened it and said, 'Oh!' There were only a pair of brushes I had purchased a few days before to enrich the appearance of my scanty personal belongings when staying in hotels. He asked to see my wallet. There were

17,000 francs in it (I believe the purchasing power was about £70 in those days). He asked me if it was my own money. I said 'Yes' and he handed it back.

I then tried to engage them in conversation—they must realize that this was very unpleasant—what would the hotel people think? They said it was nothing at all—I was apparently not used to staying in hotels (!) or I would have seen this sort of thing before—they often made 'simple verifications'. The man who was obviously the senior said that there were *fifteen* different police and security organizations now and that four or five of them, working quite independently, might well raid the hotel before next morning. He then turned to his companion and said, 'There is nothing here,' and they strode out.

I waited a couple of minutes in my room and then decided the last thing to do would be to bolt. Although they might change their minds and come back, this was a risk to be taken.

I went downstairs and into the bar again to put on a show for the benefit of any police spy who might be there. I asked the manageress what she thought of this incredible business. She laughed and said it was quite usual—there were so many police they had to find something to do. Why, only last week they had actually in this very hotel arrested and taken to the police-station for questioning a lady who had turned out to be the wife of an important police official! There had been a row about it. I noticed that as my little brush with the authorities had shown that I was not a Vichy spy of some sort, the hotel people unfroze and became quite jolly and we chatted and drank until late in the evening.

After a good night's rest I left the town the next morning. I never discovered the reason for the raid. I am inclined to believe it had nothing to do with George.

4. 'Nach Paris'

MY NEXT task was to get safely across the demarcation line. I knew that many people crossed it unlawfully and that a brisk smuggling trade had developed all along the inner frontier. The Germans were known to keep it heavily guarded, but the French authorities apparently closed their eyes to illegal crossings.

One could, I learned, cross either on foot or by some 'patent' way—hidden inside a vehicle, for instance. I heard stories of funeral processions in villages where church and cemetery were on opposite sides of the line, and where the Germans did not wonder at the large number of friends accompanying each departed one to his last resting place. The guards probably also believed that grief could completely alter the mourners' faces as they returned from the grave.

There were even 'conducted tours'. A motor-coach would drive up to the border, the passengers would get out and be led on foot across the line by a roundabout way to another coach waiting on the other side. This seemed risky to me, though it often went off quite well. Sometimes, however, the entire carload would be caught. Certain 'guides' were said to be quite unscrupulous; they would take their clients' money and then let them walk straight into the arms of a German patrol. I myself was later to discover a very good 'patent' way of crossing, in a railway locomotive. We will come to that later, but for the moment, I was in need of a lead, and spent several days trying to find one.

The penalty for an illegal crossing was a short term of imprisonment and, of course, a return to whence one came. One could also be shot at by the guards. It was essential that I should not get caught as, with my forged papers, a check on my identity would have meant the finish, so I resolved to take a bit of trouble over my first journey. I reasoned that most people would be going from north to south and vice versa. They would tend to use the direct line and cross somewhere between Loches and, say, Moulins. If the Germans were not fools this section would receive their particular attention. So, having decided against easy-looking conducted tours and funerals, I took a train southward and went to Pau. Once there I spent a few days looking round, while enjoying the splendid view of the Pyrenees from the famous terrace. I got into conversation with a number of barmen and waiters. Finally I singled out a young waiter in a large café. I went there a few times, chatted with him and tipped handsomely. Eventually I asked him if he could get me some tobacco, which he did. As we were then 'confederates in crime', I gave him to understand that I wanted to cross the line. He said he knew a man who could help and arranged a meeting. This man, who was a butcher, undertook, for a fee of 1000 francs (about £5), to accompany me right across the line. (He would only claim the money once we were safe on the other side.)

A day was set, and, while waiting, I tried discreetly to find out more about conditions in the occupied zone. One item which worried me a little was that my identity card was marked as issued from a town in the free zone and some people maintained that it would not be valid in the occupied zone unless I had an *Ausweiss* to show with it and that, if I had not, it would be presumed that I had crossed the line fraudulently.

Others said the place of issue did not matter. I was obliged to accept the latter view. Frankly, I had by now come to the conclusion that identity cards, whether genuine or well forged, were not in themselves a great stumbling-block, unless one aroused suspicion for some other reason. I knew, too, that there was a great variety of identity cards in use and it seemed unlikely that, unless there was something very obviously wrong with a card, any policeman could hope to derive much information from it at a glance. Moreover, the application of all the new measures of surveillance must have meant the enlisting of masses of inexperienced men in the various police departments and the 'fifteen' different security organizations mentioned by my inspector at Châteauroux must be cutting across each other's tracks fairly often. I had also decided to differentiate between the Vichy-created ersatz-Gestapo and the normal police and gendarmerie. It seemed unlikely that the gendarmes, trained in a military tradition, would take much pleasure in baiting their fellow-countrymen.

On the appointed day my guide and I took a motor-coach to Aire. Then we boarded another bus full of country-people with all kinds of parcels which headed towards the line. Just before reaching it we were stopped in a village by gendarmes who told us to alight and show our papers, which they inspected in a rather disillusioned manner. The sergeant who looked at my card handed it back and said, 'All right—go on—vanish!' They were obviously quite aware of our destination. They were carrying out orders to inspect our papers, but did not think it their duty to prevent Frenchmen riding about France in a motor-bus.

We all clambered back into the bus which moved off and stopped after a short distance at a barrier drawn across the road. This was the French guard post. The German one was further up the road. All the passengers jumped out and, hugging their weird assortment of luggage—some had suitcases, others boxes of various sizes and even live ducks and chickens in crates—they hurried into the fields at the roadside, while the French guards at the barrier looked on incuriously. There was an old peasant woman standing in the middle of the road shouting: 'Don't go just now. They are there waiting for you. They caught six this afternoon. Stop! You will be scuppered like rats!' No one took the slightest notice of her.

The departing passengers were filing along hedges in the fields at a good speed, but my guide shook his head and led me to a small farm a few hundred yards away. We went to the barn and he found the old farmer and a handsome young boy, a perfect specimen of the lithe, athletic Basque, from piercing eyes and eagle nose to nimble feet in his espadrilles. It was explained to me that his job was to keep slipping to and fro across the line to spot the patrols. He immediately ran off and came back a short while later to say that the bus passengers had arrived safely but that it had been a close thing and we had better wait until dusk.

We were joined by a charming couple of elderly French country-people, each about seventy years old. They had been to see some of their children who were in the free zone and had made use of the boy's services before. We all squatted down and the farmer gave us something to eat.

As night fell we sallied forth along the hedges. We wanted to reach Hagetmau, the village just across the line. When our guide signalled that we were approaching the danger zone our pace quickened. The old lady was out of breath and dropping behind and I was torn between the gallantry of slowing down and offering her my arm and an irrepressible desire to keep up with the guide and the old man. After a sprint we reached a back alley at the edge of the village and peeped around the corner into the street. After a quick glance inside a small café-hotel, the guide motioned us to enter. I gave him the 1000-franc note and he advised us to spend the night there. The last bus had gone and I would have to wait until next morning to take the early service to Dax.

I asked him if it was safe to stay in a hotel so near the line. He said yes, as the Germans did not seem to bother about the hotel and it would be better than plodding along a road in the dark. Well, it was one of those inconsistencies which kept cropping up, and I asked for a room. The old couple were also staying the night.

I went out to look at the Germans in the street. There were quite a number of them strolling about. I was surprised to see that there was a high proportion of Luftwaffe men, and tried to think where the nearest aerodrome might be.

As I sat in the café, I witnessed a little scene which seemed to come straight out of one of those hastily made and highly imaginative war plays which English producers were turning out at the time. It was as if an orthodox performance had been organized to greet me on occupied soil. The manageress of the hotel and her daughter—a sweet young girl of thirteen or fourteen—were clearing the tables when the door opened and a perfect specimen of the Teutonic superman came in. He was a big, blond-haired, pink-skinned Luftwaffe orderly in faultless uniform. He was carrying a brief-case. He clicked his heels and asked in difficult French whether they could tell him where Hauptmann somebody-or-other was. The lady and the girl immediately turned their backs and went on with their work. The superman blushed and hesitatingly repeated his question. The little girl turned her head, looked at him over her shoulder and spat out, 'What?' He became redder than ever and bit his lip, then, with wavering look asked if they would be kind enough to help him to find his officer. The mother turned; glared at him and snapped, 'Why ask us?' Then the girl said 'No', and I had never seen such hatred and contempt in so young and pretty a face. The two then shrugged their shoulders and went on clearing the tables and the young orderly slipped out into the street, redder than ever.

This was the stuff! This sweet young girl had the answer to all the politics, reasonings and false logic of Laval, Darlan and Co. That fine young fellow might have been smart and well mannered and was not causing any trouble, but he was the Boche, the enemy on their soil.

These honest country-folk saw nothing else. Their peasant instinct was telling them that no good could come of compromising with the occupation forces. No 'collaboration with the conqueror', no 'peace with honour'. This trivial incident also reassured me that the immunity of the hotel had nothing to do with any understanding between the owners and the Germans.

Early next morning I boarded a bus for Dax in the company of the old couple, several other civilians and a few German soldiers. When we arrived at Dax we went to the station to enquire about trains. The old couple were going to Arcachon and, gathering that I was new to the occupied zone, invited me to go and stay with them. I was deeply touched. This showed that

C

fooling the authorities was a passport through their outer reserve to good people's confidence.

I declined their kind offer, however, as I was in a hurry to reach Paris.

While waiting for train-time I went to explore and have a good look at the Germans. The town was full of them. Many buildings had been requisitioned and each was guarded at the entrance by a sentry standing on a small wooden platform. Wooden barriers had been set up on the pavements. Feldgendarmes (German military police) patrolled the streets in pairs with their slow, heavy gait, wearing their large half-moon-shaped badge-of-office suspended from a chain which went around the collar. The troops seemed happy, Army life and successful war obviously appealed to them. They were in their element, and I began to understand the meaning of 'war as an export product'.

I had decided to break my journey at Bordeaux and take an evening train to Paris. I preferred to arrive in the capital in the morning and have a whole day to look around and decide where to stay, rather than to arrive just before curfew-time. Bordeaux was teeming with German troops. There were also a good number of 'grey mice'—the equivalent of our A.T.S. These girls wore grey uniform and were not allowed to use make-up. Contrary to what we in England had been led to believe, the men of the Armed Forces exchanged the normal universal military salute, the girls used the Hitler salute. I discovered later that the members of the Todt organization, who wore brown uniforms, also used the Hitler salute.

As I waited for the Paris express that evening, it seemed strange to hear the announcements coming over the loudspeakers in German and French.

We arrived at the Gare d'Austerlitz in the early hours and I felt a surge of emotion at the thought of seeing Paris again. It was a grey morning and the Metro station looked bleak. I went to the centre to look at the Grands Boulevards. I shall never forget that first impression. There were too few cars to make a 'traffic roar'. The bicycles bore number-plates. The shop-windows with their shoddy displays were dark and dismal. As the French civilians walked about they seemed to ignore the Germans completely. Women clattered along on wooden-soled shoes.

Just for fun I entered two hotels reserved for Germans, then went to a small hotel near the Champs-Elysées, booked a room and left my bag. At lunch-time, I went to the restaurant in the Place des Ternes where Lucas had given me an appointment. Sure enough, there he was with some friends and he greeted me warmly. We had a good meal—this was 'semi-black market'.

Lucas gave me the news. As far as he knew, there was at the moment a total of six members of our particular organization in the occupied zone, i.e. three early arrivals, himself, Roger and Gaston, and three newcomers from our Châteauroux parachuting: my two fellow-passengers, George IX, the new radio-operator, Denis, and now myself. As George IX was our only link with H.Q., all the four others had converged towards him. Denis was out in the country, but the rest were meeting frequently in Paris. And now, as I had to use George IX also, I would be the fifth member of the 'Paris Secret Agents Club'. This get-together was most undesirable, but had been brought about by force of circumstance, so I joined.

Lucas had been able to find a safe house for George to operate his transmitter. Contact had already been made with London and a delivery of supplies requested. Lucas gave me the name and address of a bar in Montparnasse and said he would contact George and tell him to meet me there the same evening.

After lunch I went for a walk to get the 'feel' of Paris. My steps took me to the Place de l'Etoile. The colossal Arc de Triomphe in its incomparable setting looked more grandiose than ever. The unwonted quiet of the city was even more marked here. Where the seething, speeding, roaring, honking mass of traffic had swirled around the base of the great monument, before the war, the vast open space of the circular roadway was now deserted except for a few German staff cars and lorries, which looked very small in the emptiness.

I also saw a gas-driven motor-bus standing at the corner of the avenue Wagram, with its roof expanded into a huge elongated tortoise shell reaching from end to end.

As I left the Place de l'Etoile to stroll down the avenue des Champs-Elysées I heard a band in the distance. The sound was approaching from the bottom of the world-famous vista and I was soon able to distinguish a German detachment marching towards the Etoile. As it came nearer I saw it was led by an officer with drawn sword, mounted on horseback. The band was blaring out a German march and in the centre one of the musicians was carrying high a queer lyre-shaped frame decorated with horse-hair plumes and with a set of bells on which he was ringing the tune with a hammer. So this was IT! This was the unforgettable vision of German pride and domination.

The Huns had overrun many countries and were strutting all over Europe, but surely this was the supreme symbol of their conquest! They were marching up the Champs-Elysées towards the Arc de Triomphe, that unique monument to Napoleon's triumphs, on the sides of which were inscribed the names of countless German localities to testify that Germany had then been but a battleground for the victorious French.

The German servicemen who were walking on the pavement were formally saluting the troops on the march, but the French civilians were looking the other way.

On the right-hand side going down was the Hotel Astoria, from the windows of which Kaiser Wilhelm II had said he would watch the victory parade passing under the Arc de Triomphe when he won World War I. The Kaiser had neither won nor reached the Hotel Astoria. Hitler had reached the Astoria but not yet won the war. Napoleon had occupied all Europe but was defeated by the British. Hitler was occupying all Europe and had not yet defeated us, so perhaps the Germans were only having their fun while there was still time.

As I wandered on towards the Place de la Concorde, I thought that it would be also very symbolical if that particular parade got shot up. The Parisians had to endure it every day and they would enjoy seeing it scattered.

I will here anticipate to explain that I later suggested to H.Q. in London it would be a fine thing if an R.A.F. fighter could come one day and publicly blow up that hideous lyre with its bells. I gave the time-table. I have not the faintest idea whether my request had anything to do with it, but a twin-engined fighter-bomber *did* come one day early in 1942. After flying fast and low all the way from England, it suddenly appeared over the Arc de Triomphe. I was unfortunately not there on that day but I heard about it afterwards from excited spectators. They told me it arrived a few minutes too early for the parade, but roared down the Champs-Elysées below house-top level and dropped French flags on the way. When it arrived over the Place de la Concorde, it swerved and fired with its machine-guns in the direction of the Naval Ministry which was occupied by the Germans. A few nights later the R.A.F. dropped leaflets bearing photographs which had been taken by the fighter and showing the Grand Palais viewed from only a few feet above street level. It was a grand show and quite an achievement, and although it may now seem a small matter it was the forerunner of many other high-speed low-level flights by which the R.A.F. blasted the dams in Germany and sent Mosquitoes to accurately pick off selected targets without damaging the surrounding dwellings.

As I went on down towards the Louvre I began to realize what a number of Parisians had already discovered, that the charm and beauty of the city stood out much more clearly when there were no motor-cars.

I spent the next few hours looking about and trying to get used to the idea of being a Parisian again. That evening I went to the bar in Montparnasse where I was to meet George IX. From the outside it looked dreary, but it was full of people who were chattering away and looking quite gay. My arrival seemed to lower the temperature. Obviously I was worrying them because they had never seen me before. Fortunately George came in after a few minutes and we shook hands warmly. Immediately, the atmosphere unfroze. The barman lost no time in serving us, and the manager himself came up to welcome me and apologize for the frost, explaining that they had to be very careful but now that he knew I was a friend of 'Monsieur'... What could he do for us? We celebrated our reunion with a few drinks and a good dinner. I soon discovered the enormous importance of the barman during the occupation. If you wanted food, drink, tobacco, an address for a pair of shoes, a confidential message delivered to a friend, ask the barman—our Figaro of the dark days! Who has not sought his assistance? Some day a statue should be raised to *The Anonymous Barman! Largo al Factotum!* (I can see the bas-relief around the pedestal: the inside of a bar equipped with an endless row of bottles; a customer seizing a packet of cigarettes, a police inspector watching a Resistance man pocketing an envelope and a mysterious gentleman telephoning, while behind his back another mysterious gentleman listens, etc.)

That same evening I realized I would have to share another worry with the Parisians: getting home before the curfew. I noticed, as I walked through Montparnasse, that the black-out regulations were not so strict as in London, where the tiniest chink of light was pounced upon.

Certain night-clubs were allowed to remain open until morning: they could be useful if you could not get home in time. I noticed that each brothel had a notice stating whether it was requisitioned for the Germans or 'open to civilian gentlemen'. The military bureaucracy had obviously thought of everything!

I tried, during the next few days, to get the feel of my new life. In London little was known about the food situation over here. I think it could be summarized thus: in the country the peasant population could help themselves, but in the towns there was a real shortage. The quantities which escaped the regulations found their way to the black market. The opulent people who frequented bars and restaurants and had plenty of money to spend were, after all, a minority. Admitting that the town and suburban dwellers constituted 50 per cent of the population, the result was that half of the nation were going hungry and concentrating their thoughts and energies on occasionally achieving a tasty meal. The Germans had obviously planned the rationing with that in mind.

I soon came to know the 'megotorium', the little box in which one collected cigarette-butts and tobacco dust. People were not particular in those days. The worst suspicions of the origin of some of the new brands seemed to be confirmed when, in the Metro stations, one saw men carrying long poles with a small spike on the end spearing butts from between the rails. A second little box for sugar completed the average citizen's equipment.

A few days after my arrival in Paris I rented a studio in Neuilly.

5. Meeting friends

I NEXT set to work trying to organize a small circuit. Since H.Q. in London had not provided me with any contacts, I cautiously looked up some pre-war friends.

In order to avoid being recognized by other people who might know me, I generally waited for my man near his place of work and accosted him in the street. In making my selection, I proceeded entirely on the basis of judgment of his character and disregarded his pre-war political views. This principle never failed me. A former anti-British pacifist who was honest and brave could make a splendid recruit. My friend's first exclamation would be: 'Why, I thought you had got back to England! Where have you been hiding since last year?' When I explained, he was thrilled and excited. He wanted to hear more and know whether he could at last do something. We would make arrangements for my visiting his home for a talk on a day and at a time when I would not be seen by garrulous acquaintances or relations.

I soon had several places to go to.

These meetings with my friends were a great help in assessing the situation. People in the occupied zone felt very differently from those in the south. Here the invader was ever-present and collaboration could only mean treason. Industrial and business firms were controlled by German representatives. Many employees were seizing every opportunity offered by red tape to hold their contribution to a minimum.

How was it a number of French people had become collaborators? A very few had always been honestly in favour of friendship with Germany, but even some of these regretted that their chance of putting their theory into practice had only come on a victor-to-vanquished basis, but they could not escape. The vast majority of collaborators had really become such through vile, base motives. The mediocre had seized the chance of obtaining favours to overthrow their superiors. The cowardly had sought to buy reassurance from the ruthless new masters. The greedy got protections which allowed them to profiteer. The weak were eager for even the contemptuous approval of the top-dog. Second-rate journalists would say anything rather than forgo the pleasure of listening to their own voices, especially when they did not need to face contradiction. After the liberation of France, many of these pen-pushers claimed that their crime was small, as they had 'only written a few newspaper articles'. True, but as a result of those articles thousands of young Frenchmen had been fooled into making a detestable choice. A writer had, perhaps, never himself denounced a patriot, but his writings had contributed to the atmosphere which led some readers to cause their neighbours to be arrested. Full collaborators were, of course, not a majority, but they were the only publicly articulate people.

I was delighted to find that the B.B.C. bulletins were considered the only reliable source of news. In England a deep impression had been made by reports that the death-penalty was inflicted on those caught listening to our broadcasts.

The numerous war-time spy stories and espionage films had popularized the idea that the B.B.C. was being listened to only by a handful of heroes and heroines, concealed in attics, who had to dismantle and scatter the parts of their home-made receiver every time the indispensable look-out at the skylight reported a German soldier coming round the corner of the street.

Actually, one simply had to be careful that the programme was not heard from outside. I was, moreover, amazed that the German jamming never seemed to be completely effective. It was generally possible to find one or two of the several wavelengths used on which speech could just be understood. I should have thought it was possible to block any distant broadcast. Why, the lift in my pre-war home was capable of jamming out even the most powerful local stations!

General de Gaulle had much more prestige here than in the south. There could be no illusions about 'New France' and it was a great comfort to know that the French nation was still represented on the battle front.

As for Pétain, the reasoned judgment of intelligent people was that he had tried to do his best according to his own lights, but that he had been duped by his entourage, who also played on the old man's undoubted vanity.

The prestige of Winston Churchill was immense and I felt proud. We had the good fortune to have an incomparable leader who was also the greatest living orator in the world. When words were almost all we had to hurl at the enemy, he had found the right ones and spoken them with the simplicity and directness which only a complete command of the richest language ever spoken by mankind could bring. However, his theme was a simple one: 'We shall never surrender!'

In my conversations with friends, there kept recurring an ugly dreaded word, a name which had, before the invasion, sounded like part of the ritual of a demoniac creed in a remote land, but which now had acquired a meaning of sinister omnipresence: 'GESTAPO'. . . . Impossible as it had seemed a little over a year before, the Devil was in our midst. . . .

I think it is time to explain what I was expected to accomplish. Like my fellow-agents, I was to pass for an average Frenchman, while secretly organizing the sabotage of selected targets. For this, explosives, incendiary devices and weapons had to be received and delivered to the right people. The right people were those Frenchmen and Frenchwomen who wished neither to collaborate nor to wait in misery, but who felt the urge to hit and hurt the enemy in their midst, and who were prepared to take the risks involved. Beside the official, loud-voiced, arrogant world of collaboration and the sad, sullen world of official everyday life, was beginning to form the hidden, glowing world of faith and resistance. It was the privilege of a special agent to discover and recruit these fine people.

In London both the British Government and the French Government-in-exile wished to develop secret activities on French soil. They required intelligence of the German order of battle and military dispositions. Morale had to be maintained and collaboration discouraged. Direct action was to weaken the enemy and tie down his forces. Organizations were therefore created to carry out these plans and agents were trained, briefed for their various missions and infiltrated into France. Some were landed by boat or submarine on the Mediterranean coast of the unoccupied zone, a few on the northern coast of the occupied zone, a few by Lysander aircraft which actually landed inside the country, but parachuting was by far the most practical and widely used method of entering.

I do not know exactly how many agents in all had been sent before I arrived, but I believe our organization, 'F' Section, which specialized in sabotage, was one of the first in the field.

In order to receive the necessary supplies we had to find grounds in the country suitable for the dropping of containers and arrange hiding-places for weapons and explosives. When a target had been reconnoitred and a plan of attack drawn up, the explosives had to be made up into bombs and carried to those who were to do the job.

Thus each agent had to find recruits for receiving supplies, hiding them, transporting them and carrying out sabotage operations. He also needed couriers to carry messages, as the ordinary post, telegraph and telephone systems could not, of course, be trusted because of enemy scrutiny. (London was contacted by wireless, of course.)

To qualify as recruits, people had to be willing, intelligent, resolute and, above all, able to hold their tongues. This last quality was the most difficult to find. My own plan, for instance, was to ask my friends in Paris whether they knew a good man living in or near such a provincial town and who would know a number of local people. If they had someone in mind, I would ask for an introduction.

These meetings were generally gratifying experiences. As soon as he was told who I was, the man would look me straight in the eyes, offer his hand and clasping mine in a firm grip, say: 'You can count on me! What must I do?' This was the oath of loyalty. I would then take him over from my friends and make an appointment for a visit to his home town. At this second meeting I would ask whether he knew any farmers in the neighbourhood who would be willing to help with parachuting operations. He would select a couple of reliable patriots and off we would go for a ride in the country, preferably on bicycles, unless he was lucky enough to be allowed to run a car for business reasons and was in the habit of driving out to call on farmers in the neighbourhood. Building contractors, dealers in agricultural machinery, or timber merchants, for instance, could do this. Gossip flies fast in country places, civilian motor-cars were scarce and easily identifiable and it was important that our visit should not arouse curiosity. When we arrived, he would say he had brought a friend, and, in accordance with the French country tradition, glasses and a bottle of wine would be produced and we would pass the time of day with the members of the household. As soon as possible my guide would find an excuse for taking our host aside. A few moments of conversation and they would return; there would be the warm, earnest look, the strong handclasp and then the appearance of an extra-special bottle for a toast to our health and to victory. I would ask if there was a suitable dropping-ground and give the ideal specification: a clearing about 300 metres square surrounded by woods which would serve as a screen, away from roads or railway lines, and preferably on high ground so that the lights could not be seen from neighbouring hills. Yes, he could show us just such a spot. Did he know where the supplies could be hidden after reception? Yes, his own farm would be the best. He already had a secret hiding-place. It would be just the thing. Could he find a few men who could be trusted to help with the reception and the handling of the deliveries and to keep quiet about it? Yes, there was his eldest son, a cousin and a couple of boyhood friends who would be glad to help; he would answer for them.

We would then go for a walk or a ride to inspect the dropping-ground. The first one might be rejected for some fault, but he would then take us further and show us another which was acceptable. When this was settled, we would return to the farm. Our host would tell us that we could speak freely before his family as they could be relied upon to be discreet, but that if his sister-in-law, for instance, happened to call we should change the subject as she was an awful chatterbox. More refreshments would be produced and the worthy man would pour out his soul. He had fought as a young man in the 1914 war. Now the Boche and the French authorities were keeping check on his farm production and he had to give it up on requisition. However, he had always managed to conceal something (here a wink), even a few cows had not been counted! Occasionally they would secretly slaughter an odd pig for the benefit of friends and relatives. If ever we wanted some food, we only needed to come and see him. It was good to be able to do something. Weenstonn Churcheel—what a man! General de Gaulle—ah! there was a soldier—a true French-man. . . . Whatever had happened to Weygand? Why had he not gone to England? After mutual protestations of friendship and loyalty, my guide would accept a kilo of butter, a dozen eggs and a chicken and off we would go back to town.

I used to love these trips to the country. There was the exercise, the pleasure of meeting the simple sturdy country-folk, and the smell of the good earth. There were also the good meals with plenty of butter.

When we returned to my guide's home, I would ask if he knew anyone who could give reliable information about a certain target. He would promise to cautiously approach some engineer or employee who had access to the plant and see what could be done. Arrangements would be made for my spending the night there and, if I had not yet been introduced to his wife and family, I now met them. His wife would share the secret, but it would be kept from the children.

The welcome into such a home always filled me with emotion. I was, of course, a spy and a saboteur, an outlaw, a soldier without uniform engaged in forbidden warfare, and therefore fair game for the firing squad, but I was also an officer of the British Army and merely committed to danger like the rest. I was on my own in France and, from a purely personal point of view, was risking only my own skin. If hunted, I could hope to hide. With my French hosts, however, things were different. They were bound by no oath or military regulations but were running just the same risks. If things went wrong, not only the man, but his wife and young children were exposed. If the Gestapo came his home and family would be helpless. The much-advertised penalty for contact with British agents was death, to say nothing of the preliminaries. And yet I rarely saw fear in the eyes of a young wife and mother, only warmth and affection, as I would watch her turn from feeding the little ones to join in the conversation. She must have known that entertaining this guest might lead to her being torn away from her children but she had evidently put such thoughts aside. When dinner was over and the children in bed, she would bring in the coffee and say that she was happy her husband was at last able to do something as he had been making himself miserable by brooding. Then they would both start asking me about England and I would tell them how completely mobilized and determined the people were. When the time came, we would listen to the B.B.C. French broadcast and I would have to give an 'authorized' comment on the news. The fact that Hitler and Stalin, who had started the war as allies, were now fighting each other was frequently attributed to the cunning of Winston Churchill, and looked like poetic justice. It would be quite late when we retired for the night.

The next day my host would call on some of the men he had selected as prospective recruits and would report the result to me. Some had declined and were written off; but he had been success-ful with one or two others. I would by now have decided to make him my lieutenant for the area and give him a brief lecture on how to build up the circuit and keep it alive until the time came for action. I would impress on him the vital importance of secrecy. Such were the first steps in 'starting something'.

Of course this did not always work, but, as the various people along the chain were only chosen and approached after investigation by friends who had known them for some time, there were comparatively few disappointments with the first few. In this way, or at least on similar lines, small groups were being formed by various agents and for various purposes throughout the country and, as time went on, they were to grow in numbers and in size. They also sometimes came into contact with each other as I shall show later.

Another feature was the discovery of 'ready-made' groups or circuits. Some Frenchmen had already formed organizations, perhaps without clear objectives, but in the hope that sooner or later they would be reached by an agent who would provide a communication link with London and get instructions, supplies and weapons for them.

One of our contacts would approach a friend with the object of enlisting him, only to be told: 'Why, this is just what we have been waiting for! I already belong to a resistance group. It is only an organization on paper, as yet, but the chief always said something like this would happen one day and we would be able to get going.' And so a meeting in a café would be arranged as a preamble to more extended activities. Some of these 'prefabricated' groups would even have already committed acts of sabotage in a more or less efficient manner. Occasionally a Communist group would be contacted. As a rule the Communists wanted no truck with us, but would accept explosives and weapons. An agent was well-advised to be careful in his relations with an existing group as he could not know exactly how it had been formed or how good its security might be.

It must be realized that I am now writing of the late 1941–early 1942 period. Circuits formed then had to be organized so they could last for years without being 'blown'. They therefore had to be kept small, so the leader could personally supervise security and include only discreet people. Hot-headed chatter-boxes were a menace.

One of the frequent manifestations of resistance was the killing of a German soldier. The population would learn of it by the appearance of bi-lingual notices on the walls and in the Metro stations giving names of hostages who had been shot in reprisal, with a warning that worse would follow if such an act was repeated. Sometimes the list would be a long one with about twenty names.

The necessity of not causing the execution of hostages was an important consideration when planning sabotage. The unwritten rule of the game seemed to be that so long as no Germans were injured there would generally be no reprisals, although the staff could be grilled as possible accomplices, but if there were casualties among the guards, and the attackers escaped, the Germans lost no time in striking back; a group of 'political' prisoners would be hauled from their cells and slaughtered. Some of the employees of the plant might also be taken as hostages.

While on the subject of sabotage, here are a few general remarks:

The quantities of explosives or incendiaries to be used had to be so small as to be carried by a man without attracting notice or impeding his movements. Nevertheless the damage had to be crippling and put the target out of action for a long time. Pre-war films had created the popular notion of a saboteur walking past the wall of a huge factory, and throwing into the yard a bomb the size of an apple which blew the whole place to smithereens. During the blitz in Britain, however, it was found that even the several hundred pounds of explosive contained in a large aerial bomb might not do the trick. The walls and roofs could be knocked down and a number of machines wrecked; but repair and salvage gangs would get to work and a few days later the factory would be producing again. This was possible if the equipment affected could be easily repaired or replaced, and the extent to which repair work could be successful was amazing. If, however, some very special machine was destroyed and no replacement was available the whole process of manufacture could be paralysed.

The objective of the saboteur would therefore be first to find out which part of the machinery was vital and then get into the factory and put it out of action, by smashing one of its components which could be neither repaired nor replaced for a long time.

The pound or so of high explosive would have to be applied in firm contact with the parts. Such a small quantity produces little blast effect and metals are not much affected by blast anyway. Direct contact is essential for the transmission of the explosion shock-wave, which has the effect of a tremendous shattering hammer-blow. This effect will be lost if there is even only a small gap left between explosive and metal or if some soft material is interposed. Obviously the saboteur must know exactly where and how he must place the charge, so that reliable information had first to be obtained. Moreover, if the result was not a complete success at the first attempt, there might well be no second chance as the futile bang would cause the enemy to investigate the security of that particular plant, and perhaps discover and plug up the loopholes which the saboteur had used.

The same necessity for effectiveness applies to any target. Let us take as an example a familiar object: a steam locomotive. These were very important targets as massive transport depended on them. Place a small bomb against the side of the boiler and the result will only be a hole in the thin metal sheeting surrounding the heat-insulating lagging which forms a soft layer around the boiler-wall proper. Place it on a wheel or connecting rod and it will be powerless against the massive steel forging or casting. Put it in among the coal so that it gets shovelled into the furnace and the result may be damage to the fire-box which can be repaired in a local workshop, etc., etc. But place it against the bare end of a steam cylinder and the locomotive may be out of action for months and months. This is because these cylinder ends are made of cast iron and therefore easily shattered. Also, as they are parts which do not normally wear out, very few spares are kept by the

D

railway companies and it may take them a long time to have replacements manufactured.

There were many ways of effecting sabotage without using explosives and these also required some know-how to be effective. Before leaving England agents were given instruction in these matters and it was their job to teach the recruits in the field. This was important as, apart from the result itself, we did not want to have good men risk their lives for nothing. For instance, it had been announced that all over Europe patriots were paralysing transport by putting handfuls of sand into the axle-boxes of railway waggons and thus causing them to seize up. Some experts in England tried the experiment and found that it had no effect whatever—the wheels just kept on turning. They then studied the various types of French axle-boxes and told us how to do it. . . .

Thanks to our training we were quite well informed on these matters, but unfortunately it was to be a long time before my friends and I were able to become really active as I shall recount.

As I have explained, I met Lucas frequently in Paris and we used to discuss another subject: that of the enemy forces arrayed against us. During our training we had attended lectures on the organization of the German Armed Forces and security organizations. There seemed to be roughly two branches of the latter; first the purely military intelligence, counter-espionage and police, which reported to the High Command of the Wehrmacht, and secondly the State or Nazi security service (Sicherheitsdienst), of which the legendary Gestapo was a part and which reported to the Supreme Command, that is to the Führer through Himmler. All this was very interesting, but in the streets of Paris what we might meet were not diagrams on blackboards, but hefty fellows with pistols and handcuffs, so we were more concerned with the practical aspect of not having anything to do with them, whichever particular department they might belong to.

There were also the French police who dealt with ordinary common crime, the enforcement of the myriad regulations and offences against the Vichy administration. Naturally, the Germans could control them also in the occupied zone, and examine their prisoners to see whether there was a possible security aspect to any particular case. If, for instance, the French detained a man on the suspicion that he was a black-market operator and found evidence that he was a member of a resistance group, they were supposed to hand him over to the Germans.

Individual French police-officers were frequently loath to do this and might try to save the man but, although they sometimes succeeded, this was not always possible as the Germans had their informers who kept watch. There were also some police-officers who were collaborators and those who had the Vichy mentality. In addition the Gestapo employed directly a number of ex-police-inspectors. Such renegades were very valuable as they knew their fellow-countrymen.

We also had to reckon with the swarm of spies and informers who spied on the garrulous, the boastful and the unwary. My picture of the detective as a disciple of Sherlock Holmes solving problems by astute deduction was replaced by the vision of a rough-neck bureaucrat sitting at a desk, reading reports and listening to the tittle-tattle of narks and traitors.

The difficulty with the secret network is that one arrest might lead elsewhere and a whole group of people eventually be taken as a result of suspicion aroused by one, as a ball of wool can be unrolled by drawing on one end. As for interrogation: the twentieth century will unfortunately go down in history as having perfected the techniques of torture. But let us leave this depressing subject for a while to travel a little. . . .

Our radio-operator, George, had left Paris late in October 1941 and moved to Le Mans. He had been operating from a studio flat and thought that some inquisitive person had peeped in one day and seen his set. Also, he was having difficulty in making contact with home. Lucas, who had a group in the Le Mans area, found another place for him. Lucas had ordered a delivery of supplies and directed that this first dropping of containers should take place near a village called Vaas, halfway between Le Mans and Tours. As this was a kind of experimental operation, I asked that some stuff for myself be included in the delivery and agreed to Lucas's proposal that I go personally to superintend the reception. So I went by train to Vaas where I met George at the house of the schoolmaster, M. Besnier, who was an ardent patriot. The reception committee was to consist of Besnier, a farmer friend of his and myself. It was all very small and modest, but such were our first efforts. I believe this was the first time, or at least one of the first times, that a B.B.C. 'personal message' was used. The principle was that the R.A.F. could not possibly guarantee that an aircraft would fly to a particular place on a fixed date. First, the weather conditions had to be right, both at night over the target area and especially when the plane returned to land in England in the early morning. Secondly, very few aircraft were committed to these operations in those days.

The drill had therefore consisted until then in having the reception committee stand by every night from the beginning of the 'moon-period'—about three nights before full moon. The plane might arrive any night until three or four nights after full moon. If it failed to do so the operation would be put off until the next moon-period, three weeks later. For instance, when I had made the journey myself, I had been due to leave during the early-August moon-period, but every evening for a week the flight had been scrubbed and then postponed until the early-September moon. Even then it was only on the third or fourth day that we flew (I may add that this waiting to jump from one evening to the next was a disagreeable business and we used to call it 'being crucified').

Now it was very inconvenient for the reception committee to be out every night for a whole week and difficult for the radio-operator to listen for a message every evening at about 8 p.m. and get the news to the men in time. It was therefore arranged that the reception committee should receive the signal themselves. An agreed 'personal message' was given at the end of the B.B.C. evening broadcasts to France on the day when the plane was coming. It was broadcast twice, first at 7.30 p.m., as a warning to prepare for that night, and again at 9.15 p.m., as confirmation that the aircraft was actually leaving. If it came over on the first broadcast, but not on the second, it would mean that the operation had been planned for that night, but that the last meteorological report received an hour before take-off had been bad and the flight belatedly cancelled. Thus the various members of the reception committee could be forewarned in their own homes. I seem to remember that our first message was 'Pierre is well' if the operation was 'on' and that we even had the luxury of a cancelling message 'Pierre sends greetings' if it was scrubbed. The result of this perfect arrangement was that I spent several days enjoying the hospitality of M. and Mme Besnier, and being cheered up by their contagious enthusiasm and glowing patriotism, but every evening 'Pierre' sent his damned greetings and I finally had to go back to Paris with nothing but the pleasant memory of a few days in the country with charming friends. Yet the moon had shone brightly on several nights and George had sent a signal to H.Q. stating that if they were waiting for the midnight sun, this did not appear in France. . . .

I met Lucas and in return for my 'nil' report, he had news— and bad news. A 'refugee' named Christophe had arrived in Paris from the unoccupied zone with a tale of woe.

6. The tame locomotive

IN EARLY October 1941, during the moon-period which followed my own arrival, four new agents had been dropped near Périgueux. This time it had not been a very neat operation, police patrols had been sent out and one of the 'bodies' caught the next day. The other three had got clear, proceeded to Marseilles, and gone to Christophe's home, which address had been given to them as a safe house where they could find a means of communicating with H.Q. in case anything went wrong. Unfortunately the Vichy police had been tipped off and laid a trap. Christophe told us he himself had barely escaped being caught in his own house, and he had been unable to warn the others.

Our informant had also learned through the grapevine that, in addition to the three new agents, several other people had been caught in this mousetrap. Among them were George Noble, our first radio-operator, who had received us near Châteauroux, and who had later disappeared. Trott and Marcel, two of my flying-companions, and Gerald, whom I had met at Châteauroux.

I remember Lucas and myself giving some of our precious food coupons to this survivor of the disaster.

Of course, the fate of the others was none of our business, as we were to work separately, but it did show the terrible weakness created when agents were in touch with each other. The moral of it all was that each organizer must have his own wireless-operator and we resolved to press H.Q. for more of these men.

Here in the occupied zone the necessity of being in touch with our only link, George IX, was still keeping Lucas, Roger,

Gaston, Denis and myself in the 'Paris Club'. However, it had to go on until H.Q. provided more 'Georges'.

I returned to making contacts of my own in preparation for the time when I should be able to receive deliveries. I moved around quite a bit. I used to meet Lucas and Roger regularly in Paris. One day Roger took me to lunch at Maxim's. This famous restaurant was a favourite haunt of the German 'Big Brass' (Goering is said to have gone there when he was in Paris). When we walked in we were ushered upstairs, and the maître d'hôtel led us to a table away from the window and put a screen half around us. There was certainly plenty of 'Big Brass' sitting at the other tables.

Roger proceeded to order a meal with the discrimination and seriousness which only a Frenchman can command on such an occasion. We were trying Maxim's because it was one of the famous 'Six' where you could, if you wished, legally blow a whole month's ration tickets on one sumptuous meal. The food and service were marvellous. We had to take a look at the German generals every now and then to realize there was a war on.

Halfway through the meal, while refilling our glasses, the imposing 'sommelier' suddenly said in an undertone: 'It is a real pleasure to serve Frenchmen. These gentlemen take great pains to appear distinguished, but after the third course, the pig begins to show.' I wondered why he made this remark, he did not know us from Adam. It is said a good head-waiter can sense the character of a client. I was only hoping his intuition would not be too good! I could feel the resentment of this dignitary of the table at the idea that the best of French foods and wines were going down the Boche gullets.

It was November and very cold. There was practically no heating. In private homes people were burning all kinds of ersatz fuels, such as sawdust. There were advertisements for small collapsible cubicles with windows in the sides, which could be set up around a group of four people sitting at a small table, to keep their animal heat inside. In my flatlet there was a drop of lukewarm water on Sunday morning, but only cold all the rest of the week. For most people shivering was added to hunger. From the German point of view there were two sides to it: on the one hand, it kept the population busy grubbing for warmth as well as food, but, on the other hand, it made them more resentful. I often discussed the 'art of occupation' with my friends, and began to get an idea of what had occurred since the collapse in June 1940. The Nazis had been represented as savage monsters, but when they arrived they looked just like soldiers, and very smart ones too. They had not at first interfered much with the return home of those who had fled southwards. For a short while the demarcation line had been left very open. They did not pester women. It took some time to get their controls in position and functioning. They had even taken many more prisoners than they should have done, by giving out that captives would be merely kept in P.o.W. enclosures for a short while and then sent home. In fact, listening to them, one received the impression that the cages were de-mobilization centres and French soldiers would be well advised to surrender and get the formalities over, whereas if they escaped south it would take much longer to legalize their status. Many believed that such an agreement had been made with Marshal Pétain and a number of soldiers had thus been tricked into allow-ing themselves to be rounded up by very small squads.

Once the Germans had organized their military establish-ments, however, things had changed. Prisoners were sent to Stalags and Oflags in Germany, the demarcation line became a real frontier, restrictions were slapped on and the Gestapo got busy. In short, the occupation had started with the velvet glove, but the steel claws had soon emerged and the grip gradually tightened, so that incipient resistance soon began to harden.

France is a modern nation whose economic life depends on a number of large towns with industrial suburbs. The excellent rail and road systems are ideal for swift transport. If an invader, who has acquired a reputation of invincibility by winning battles in record time, occupies such a country and has the sense to refrain from driving the population too far, it is not difficult to ensure a large measure of control. At the time of which I am writing conscription of Frenchmen for forced labour in Germany had not yet been introduced. When this was enforced, later on, thousands of men went into hiding in the woods and hills and formed the famous Maquis. This was to be an example of the occupying power going too far.

In the winter of 1941-2, however, the organizers of resistance were starting business in a modest way. For instance, when I had left England I had been given a sum of only 26,000 francs, the purchasing power of which was about £100, and this for a stay of indefinite length. No contacts were given for receiving more money. One does not need to be a specialist on subversive activities to realize that this was on the inadequate side.

Actually, money was running short when, in the middle of November, Lucas told me he was worried. There had been no news from Le Mans for several days. He feared George might be in trouble. As I seemed to be very mobile, would I care to go and cautiously make enquiries? He gave me the address of the brother of M. Besnier of Vaas, who lived in Le Mans; he also belonged to the group and might know what had happened.

I went and found him. He said George had been arrested. There were conflicting rumours on how it had occurred, but there it was. George had obviously not talked, as there seemed to have been no repercussions. I returned to Paris and gave Lucas the bad news.

There were two possibilities: either H.Q. would guess the situation when George ceased to transmit and try to send a messenger to Lucas, or we could try to get a message to London ourselves to ask for another operator. A few days later Lucas was beaming happily. He had had the good luck to find another un-expected radio-link with London. This was his story. He had made a number of contacts in Paris. One of these, a lawyer, had met a lady who was doing resistance work already. Lucas had been introduced to her and she revealed that she was a member of an espionage network which had been formed by a refugee Polish officer and which was in touch with London through their own secret wireless-transmitter. The organization had been 'blown' and its chief and most of its members arrested. There were, however, a few survivors, including herself and the wire-less-operator, who were lying low. She was delighted at the good luck of meeting Lucas, and the remnants of her group could become active again.

Lucas had asked her to transmit a message to London asking for money. She brought him a reply. He left for Vichy where an important person representing a neutral country handed him the sum required. Contact had been re-established! Another message was sent asking for new wireless-operators, but when the reply came it stated that they had no men trained and ready to leave and we must be patient. I chose not to use this means of communication myself and to wait until a new operator arrived from home before asking for deliveries of supplies for my own group.

I had been given an interesting contact in the unoccupied zone and I decided to make a return trip across the demarcation line. I wanted a better way of getting across than buses and walking and one of my friends, an engineer named Nel Marcorelles, told me of the very thing. He owned a country house near Montauban, in the free zone, and employed a young servant-girl. She used to have food sent from Bordeaux. It was smuggled across the line by acquaintances of hers who were the driver and fireman of the Bordeaux-Marseilles express. One day they had said that if she wanted to make the journey herself they could smuggle her across as well. She had accepted and been taken to the locomotive depot, lifted into a recess under the tender, and thus been trans-ported all the way between Montauban and Bordeaux. This method sounded very attractive; and as it had been discovered by a young, simple servant-girl, and not organized by some Master-Mind of an Intelligence Service, I decided it was probably quite safe and reliable. I was given the address of the fireman and took the evening express to Bordeaux.

As there had been no time to send advance notice of my arrival, I would have to talk my own way into the confidence of the engine crew, my only introduction being the girl's name. As

I sat in the train all night, I inwardly rehearsed ingratiating overtures and disarming smiles.

When I arrived in Bordeaux in the morning I made my way to the address and found a small house in a little street near the marshalling-yard. I rang and a lady opened the door. I produced my smiles and honeyed words and was ushered in. I was lucky as the fireman was at home. He listened to my request and nodded. They asked no questions. He said he would take me across with the evening express. His locomotive was hauling it as far as Montauban. I could come back to this house in the evening and have supper with them and he would lend me some overalls, as it would be a dirty journey for me.

I spent the day walking about the town and returned at the appointed hour. I shared their simple meal and my host brought in the driver. They were both very friendly. They had accepted the girl's name as an introduction, and were going to play the game. There were still no questions asked.

At dusk I donned the overalls and the three of us left the house and walked on to the footbridge which spanned the great network of rails forming the marshalling-yard. We passed the watchman's post and at the other end went down the steps to the engine depot. All around were goods trains being formed and shunted. There were French and German railway employees and armed German soldiers sitting on top of some of the open goods-waggons. There were other overalled locomotive-crews moving to and fro, and we reached our engine without attracting notice. We stopped beside the tender. Another engine standing alongside hid us from the view of the guards. The tender was a huge affair, far bigger than the British models.

In France, there do not seem to be as many water-trough facilities for picking up water while running as at home, and the locomotives have to take greater volumes of it with them. Moreover, their all-steel carriages are heavier and the engines must be more powerful than ours.

After a quick look round, they pushed me between two of the wheels under the tender. I looked up and saw that I was crouching under a cavity in the bottom of the water-tank. All along the tender the bottom was resting on the chassis girders, except for this gap about two feet long and six feet wide in the under-surface. It could be seen only from underneath as the side walls of the tender were continuous. (Incidentally, I have never been able to discover the reason for this particularity in the design. It seemed to have been made for British spies!)

I climbed up on to the chassis girders, into the cavity, and found that it was about two feet high. My friends pushed some wooden planks up and I manœuvred them under me across the girders, to form a floor to my tiny compartment. There were wide gaps between the planks through which I could see some of the wheels and axles and the rails and sleepers. I could not sit up, but could lie down quite comfortably on the planks. As these were laid flat, there was no danger of falling out.

After a while there was a groaning sound and the wheels began to turn. We were moving backwards. I saw switch-points passing below, then I felt the brakes being applied, we moved dead slow and stopped with a gentle bump. We had backed on to the train.

The sounds from the station were coming up through my floor. After a few minutes the wheels began to turn forwards and we were off. We clanked and bumped over switch-points for a couple of minutes and then were running smoothly over the main line. It was quite dark outside by now and I could occasionally see a glow from the ash-box under the furnace. We gathered speed gradually and soon the sleepers were rushing below in a dim blur.

It was something like lying in the plane which had brought me over . . . but at a considerably lower altitude, of course! I decided there and then that if all went well this time I would use this as my normal passage across the line. After a run of thirty or forty minutes the brakes came on and we ground to a standstill. This must be Langon, the last station on the occupied side, and the point at which the Germans searched the train. There was a fifty-minute stop while they did this. Several times the rails and ballast below were illuminated as if by lamps shone under the tender. There was much coming and going, but I felt quite safe in my little box.

Finally whistles blew, the wheels began to turn again, and we gathered speed. A few minutes later we slowed down and stopped once more. This must be La Réole, the first stop in the unoccupied zone. A torch-light shone under me and the voice of the driver came up through the planks: 'You can come out now and finish the journey with us in the cab!' I stood the planks on edge and passed them down to him. I then dropped between the chassis girders on to the ballast and wormed my way out between the wheels. We both climbed the steps up to the lighted footplate between the bewildering array of levers and dials of the loco-motive and the coal-bunker of the tender. I asked whether the presence of a third man on the engine would not be remarked. My friends said there were no Germans here and that if anyone asked questions they would say I was a railway engineer making a check-run, and tell him to go to blazes. The starting signal was given, the driver spun the valve-wheel, pulled the throttle-lever and we moved ponderously off.

My boyhood dream had come true! I was riding on the foot-plate of an express engine! The fireman was stoking the furnace. I pressed into a corner behind the driver on the left-hand side of the cab out of the way of the shovel. Through the open fire-door I could see beyond the incandescent gas right to the front of the long fire-box. The fireman had to fling the shovelfuls of coal so they were spread evenly over the entire surface of the grate. It was quite an art. It also required strength and stamina as there could be few pauses for rest. Five or six tons of coal had to be fed to the raging fire in about three hours' running time. We went faster and faster and the noise grew. The needle of the Flaman indicator-recorder in front of the driver crept up to seventy, eighty, ninety, a hundred kilometres an hour. A muffled throbbing came from the funnel up in front. Behind I could see the roof of the first carriage bobbing about in the blackness above the top of the tender. The springs of an engine are hard and the cab was swaying and bumping noisily.

The crew realized I was a locomotive enthusiast and proudly exhibited their beloved baby. They showed me the poor-quality lubricating-oil which was being issued to them—horrible stuff —not even fit for a bicycle! The coal was not what they were used to, either. Yes, it was a fine locomotive, a great Pacific, a four-cylinder compound; it could develop over 2000 h.p. It weighed 100 tons alone and the tender full of water and coal seventy tons. No wonder the Boches were taking many of these to Germany! I checked myself from shouting above the din that some friends and I were going to attend to precisely this very matter. Occasionally I pushed my head out over the side into the gale of wind to look ahead into the night. All I could see were the coloured signal lights. One of the things which seem strange to a layman on a locomotive at night is the rushing into a black void. There are no headlights to illuminate the track as on a car.

I noticed that from time to time the driver would pull on a short chain which hung in front of him. He explained that this was 'la vigilance'. He had seen a light meaning that a 'distant' or warning signal was closed against him. He pulled this chain to make a mark on the chart which was enclosed within the speed-indicator and on which the whole history of the journey was being recorded automatically. When the signal was passed a trip mechanism would make another mark on the chart. The chart would later be removed and inspected by the supervisors and, if his own mark was not found preceding that made by the signal, he would be put on the mat and accused of not having noticed the signal. If he passed a closed 'stop' signal, not only would there be a mark on the paper, but a mighty alarm-whistle would sound in the cab and even if, thanks to this, no accident occurred, there would be the very dickens of a row and stiff penalties when the chart was examined. (When reading accounts of inquiries into railway accidents in Britain, even several years after the war, I was astonished to learn that our own engines were not fitted with these simple yet effective devices.)

We stopped several times on the way to Montauban. At each

station the train came to rest along the lighted platform, with the engine just beyond in the shadow. There we could wait calmly until the fuss died down and the guard's whistle allowed our powerful steed to move again.

I fell to thinking what a wonderful fundamental organization a railway is. Every modern nation depends for its life on its railways more than on anything else. Railwaymen are a well-trained, perfectly disciplined body of men of high professional standard. They run their special world of steel and motion in a thoroughly conscientious manner. Here in France they had realized that the survival of the country depended on maintaining train services, and although the idea that the railways were used extensively by the enemy was anathema to them and they loathed the presence of German employees, they knew this had to be accepted if they were to keep their own trains running and were carrying on. The expresses were running to time, the food-trains were getting through, the carriages were kept clean and, even in the dining-cars, the food was better value for money than in most restaurants in those days.

As time went on some of the finest resistance activities were to be those of the railwaymen. There were precious few collaborators under the S.N.F.C. badge!

We arrived at Montauban station late at night and were uncoupled from the train to be replaced by an electric locomotive. We shunted back and forth and wound up in the engine depot. My friends banked the fire and did a few other chores, and we finally climbed down from the cab and slipped out of the yard through a wicket-gate.

We went to a small café where I returned the overalls and tried to clean up. I was not oily, but covered with rust from the sides of my hiding-place. My friends would accept no reward whatever, except a couple of glasses of beer.

We made an appointment for the next day. I went to an hotel and spent some time trying to get the rust out of my skin before going to bed. The next morning more rust kept coming out of my pores. I thought I should never be clean again.

When I met my friends, Mademoiselle Edwige, my fairy-godmother of this magic carpet, was with them. She was young and charming. Means of contacting them at either end for future journeys were agreed upon and they still asked no questions.

I had told them I was a friend of Edwige's employer, and his name opened all doors to me; I had their confidence. They still refused to accept any reward.

I was to use this 'tame' railway engine as long as the demarcation line remained an obstacle. I heard that the Germans did eventually have suspicions, but I understand that, although they made several thorough searches, they never caught anyone in that tender.

In the free zone, I felt relief at the absence of green uniforms. Here one saw only an occasional car containing a German officer with an orderly chauffeur, probably on some liaison mission. There was no curfew to worry about and the black-out regulations were not strictly enforced. On the other hand, the food situation seemed worse than in the occupied zone. For one thing, the Germans were sitting on the richest parts of the land, and also the busybody Vichy officials were more zealous in pestering their fellow-countrymen in the name of the new brand of patriotism.

In railway trains and hotels the frequency of routine identity-card checks increased. I found the best attitude to adopt for these was the kind of sulky truculence a fed-up Frenchman would feel at all this poppycock (too pleasant a manner might suggest hiding something). People who have wearied of my friendship have said this must have come quite naturally to me!

I was in Marseilles when the *Repulse* and *Prince of Wales* were sunk, and the Japanese attacks on Pearl Harbour brought the United States into the war. The reaction in France was that the course of events was beginning to take on a strange resemblance to that of World War I.

I attended to my business and set out again for Paris. One of the men I had recruited during my trip, on the recommendation of Nel, had told me of a convenient way of crossing the line near Ribérac. As I was on the look-out for every possibility, I decided to experiment with it instead of returning on the locomotive this time.

I went to Ribérac by bus and walked to a house on the outskirts where a woman told me the route to follow. I proceeded alone down a path, over a hedge, up a slope, through a farmyard, past a barking dog, through a field, along a path and joined a main road on the other side.

A walk of a mile or so brought me to a village where I found a bus for Montmoreau. There I took a local train to Angoulême and changed to an express for Paris. It had been easy. I was to learn later, however, that the very man who had told me about this passage, was caught himself a few days afterwards while using it. The guards took him before an officer. He fortunately spoke German fluently, being an Alsatian, and had played the sentimental chord, saying he was going to spend Christmas with relatives. The German officer interrogated him closely and then said that, as an Alsatian, he would soon have the honour of becoming a citizen of the German Reich, so he would not send him to prison, but back to where he came from. My friend refrained from telling him that the 'relative' he was going to see was an English 'cousin' in Paris. So it appeared I had been lucky and that the locomotive was really the best and quickest way.

E

7. The 'Victoire' affair

I saw Lucas on my return and he said the ex-Polish radio-link was still working with London and that another attempt to drop supplies at Vaas was to be made during the next moon-period. He was going there himself. Mme Carré, the lady he had recently met, had introduced him to another survivor of the Polish organization—a Belgian business man who had managed to procure a permit to drive a car—and they were all three going by road.

I was hoping that it would soon be possible to become active. My recruits were waiting. However, this matter of radio-communication with London had to be cleared up first. The ex-Polish transmitter was a godsend, but there were too many intermediaries handling the messages and I had never seen the operator. I should have preferred to give him my messages myself.

Just before Christmas I met Lucas again and he told me he had been to Vaas with his friends, but the aircraft had not appeared and it was another wash-out.

I spent Christmas Eve with Monsieur and Madame Brun, good friends of mine for years. The special circumstances of our reunion and the secret we shared created an unforgettable warmth and depth of feeling, one which cannot be equalled in ordinary life.

It was otherwise a gloomy time for our group. No weapons, no money. As I had no warm clothing, one night I went and burgled the flat in Boulogne-sur-Seine, where I had lived before the collapse. I had ascertained that it was unoccupied. It was strange to creep up the familiar stairs in stockinged feet with shoes tied around the neck. I did not linger. The electricity had been cut off and I dared not light my pocket-lamp. The moonlight lit up my skis, which had somehow found their way to the kitchen.

Just before New Year Lucas arranged a lunch, to which Roger, Gaston and myself were invited to meet the helpful Mme Carré. It was a cheerful reunion in a de-luxe black-market restaurant. The lady was slim and pleasant, but very short-sighted. She apparently considered that wearing glasses would spoil her looks and constantly peered at us from puckered eyelids. She told us what a catastrophe it was that 'Armand', her Polish chief, and most of his network had been taken, and how lucky she and a few others had been to escape. She was very happy to meet us, and was very talkative. She rejoiced in the code name of Victoire and the nickname of 'La Chatte'. She obviously liked the company of men and loathed other women. She appreciated blue funny stories. I had a collection of these. (In fact at home there had been a libellous rumour that I had been promoted to commissioned rank chiefly so that the officers' mess could be entertained by them.) The lunch was a great success.

A message had been received from London over her transmitter saying that they would attempt to succeed with the Vaas operation during the next moon, and that this time they would also drop two agents, one of whom would be a wireless-operator with a new transmitter. This was better.

The days dragged by in the bitter cold. I used to make a point of not staying in my lodgings during the day as it would not do to appear idle. I went to the cinema quite a bit. Some German films were not too bad. We were also treated to lengthy war newsreels. Whereas in England we saw gun-sight views of Messerschmitts going down in flames, in Paris we were shown only Hurricanes and Spitfires being riddled by tracer bullets. It was the opposite point of view!

I have often been asked whether my speech ever gave me away. Before the war I did speak French with an English accent.

In preparation for my trip I had practised pronouncing the 'r's' from the throat as the French generally do and my friends had said that I sounded just like a Frenchman from the eastern provinces. Of course, some recruits did say I had an accent, but it was only after they were let in on the secret and exposed to auto-suggestion. Only three people—a barman, an ethnologist and an optician—ever spontaneously asked me if I was English. The barman was obviously used to sizing up his international clientele. The ethnologist, whom I met quite by chance, had been an explorer and was employed as an expert at the anthropological museum at the Palais de Chaillot in Paris. He began by pointing out with much gesticulation, his hands drawing various geo-metrical figures in the air before my face, that my cheekbones and eyebrows (I have forgotten the actual morphological terms he employed) showed a formation frequently found in English types. When I remarked that all European races were mixed, he exclaimed, 'But, *bon Dieu*! He has the accent also, he will surely be arrested!' The only thing left for me to do was order another round of drinks in my very best 'argot'—after all, there was no shame in being spotted by such a distinguished expert.

There may have been a little auto-suggestion in the case of the optician. I wore no disguise in France. I believe it was John Buchan who, in *Thirty-Nine Steps* laid down that a disguised spy could *look* different and be the same, but an undisguised one could look the same and *be* different.

None the less, and in order to reduce the chances of being recognized, I one day decided to acquire a pair of horn-rimmed spectacles, as these can alter the look of the eyes. I did not need glasses at all, but could not very well ask for plain-glass windows, so I said my eyesight was good but I felt a little tired sometimes when reading, and asked for the very lowest power. As the optician was fitting the lenses, he suddenly asked: 'Are you an Englishman?' I replied: 'Of course not. How could I be?' 'Oh, well, I thought that perhaps . . .' He added nothing more.

I have often been asked whether I accidentally met and was recognized by pre-war friends whom I had no reason for wishing to see. This did occur. If I thought he might be of use, I spoke to him. If not, I walked on without a sign of recognition. Some obviously recognized me, others thought they were mistaken. The friends I had let into the secret would warn me about meeting certain pre-war acquaintances, as these were hand-in-hand with the Germans. I did not expect that any of these would call out to the feldgendarmes on sight, but they would tell a number of other people. I did not know how efficient the Gestapo were, but I had to allow for the case of their being very thorough.

When the moon-period came I went to Vaas. We all thought M. Besnier's patience was finally going to be rewarded, when the long-awaited message at last came in on both B.B.C. programmes. We went to the dropping-ground. At midnight we heard the drone of a plane in the distance and lit three torch-lamps as a recognition signal. The droning kept growing louder and then fading away. The aircraft was obviously circling around a wrong spot several miles away. After half an hour the sound died away altogether. We waited another hour, but could hear only the chuffing of a locomotive and the clanking of goods-waggons over at Mayet station, so we left the ground sorely disappointed. For the rest of the period there was nothing but 'greetings from Pierre', so I returned to Paris with another 'nil' report.

A few days later Lucas declared that parachuting was obviously unreliable in winter and asked whether I could organize an M.T.B. landing on the north coast. I approached Nel Marcorelles for a contact and again he had the very thing. A cousin of his, Monsieur Bousquet, hastened to Brittany and returned with an ideal set-up: a patriotic friend of his owned a villa near Moulin-de-la-Rive—a small beach between Lannion and Morlaix. He also had a motor-lorry which we could use for transporting our supplies. Just the job! I felt this would be as good as the tame locomotive at Montauban.

It was galling to think that, having these excellent contacts, I had been so far unable to get any supplies at all.

I gave the location of the landing-beach to Lucas for transmittal to London with a request that the long-overdue delivery be switched from air to sea. London advised that it would be laid on as suggested and confirmed that two agents, one of them a radio-operator, would be landed.

Whereas air drops needed a bright moon, beach landings required total darkness and the operation was fixed for February 12th at midnight. The thaw had come, we were no longer suffering from the cold and things were beginning to look brighter. It was, however, to be but the lull before the storm!

One day late in January I met Roger, who had a message from Lucas asking us both to meet him for dinner at a certain restaurant. We all three arrived at about the same time. Lucas was wearing a grave look. We ordered our meal and when the waiter had laid the first course before us, Lucas leaned forward and began:

'I am afraid I have some very, very bad news. . . .' A pause. 'As you know, Victoire's story was that when the Polish organization was blown, she and a few others escaped arrest. Well, that is not true. . . . She was caught too!' Roger and I watched him. 'But keep on eating; it will look more natural.' We got busy with knives and forks.

'She seems to be running around quite free,' I said. 'How did she give them the slip?' Lucas drew a deep breath. 'That's just the trouble. She didn't. . . . No! . . . *She agreed to work for them as a double agent and has given us away!*'

According to tradition, I should have felt a tingling of the scalp, a quickening of the pulse, a sickness in the pit of the stomach. After all, it is not every day that you get this kind of news flung at you. However, I felt just nothing at all at first, and found myself stuffing another forkful of *pommes de terre à l'huile* into my mouth.

Then my next obvious question: 'But what about the radio messages? I suppose they were just a lot of hooey?' 'No, they were genuine enough. . . . You see, they got the set and the encoder . . . and are keeping the game going, communicating with London. . . . Victoire has been very valuable to them. . . . She composes the right kind of messages, just as if nothing had happened. The messages I wrote and the replies we received were transmitted faithfully, *but under the supervision of a Feldwebel.*'

I ruminated on this for a while. 'Then they must have been following us and have found out about all our contacts.' 'Not all, I think, but some, of course.'

Lucas proceeded to tell us all he knew, while we tried to look and behave as if we were chatting normally.

Victoire's wretched confession ran more or less as follows:

Victoire had been arrested shortly after her chief by a squad led by a secret-police officer named Hugo Bleicher and locked up in the Santé Prison. This Bleicher had forced her to go with them to the various bars and cafés where surviving members of the organization had arranged to meet, and she had witnessed the capture of a number of the poor fellows. Having thus been pitchforked into co-operation under duress and the threat of a return to the Santé, she agreed to the suggestion that she should become a double agent. She was then set free. Her new status included the appointment of mistress to Herr Bleicher. Her day-time job consisted in spying and reporting on suspects. It was quite easy for her to maintain her pose as an escapee from the Armand catastrophe. One of her trusting acquaintances was the lawyer who also knew Lucas and who had made the introduction.

She reported him to Bleicher who gave her orders to worm her way into his organization and find out all about it. The possibility of sending W/T messages to London was an irresistible bait and had certainly landed a big one! Lucas had established that there was no possible doubt about the radiograms received in reply to his own being genuine transmissions by our H.Q. in London. Victoire had produced one or two of her friends, including the 'Belgian business man' who was fortunate enough to have a car and who had driven Lucas and the lady to Vaas. *This was none other than Bleicher himself!* Even the restaurant where we had enjoyed our New Year reunion was one of Bleicher's favourite eating-places, and his henchmen, whom we had taken for innocent diners, had had a good look at us!

As Lucas proceeded with his story, the implications of the

situation began to take shape. For instance, the forthcoming sea operation in Brittany was being arranged through the good offices of the Germans! Poor Lucas was suffering intensely. What we had thought was an extraordinary bit of luck had turned out to be a trap, ready to close on us all.

And why had Victoire decided to confess? Because a few seemingly minor details such as the delay in the transmission of a message or an inconsistency had aroused Lucas' curiosity: also, a couple of more serious matters (the arrest of a friend, the procuration by Victoire of over-perfect false papers bearing genuine German stamps) had strengthened his doubts. Someone had also given a hint to the lawyer that all might not be well with her. Anyway, Lucas had challenged her suddenly and she had broken down and told the wretched truth. He could, of course, have killed her on the spot, but decided not to. It was vital, for the sake of the others, to find out the extent of the damage and to gain time. He decided that her repentance was sincere and that her obvious megalomania and shame at having given way to the Germans could be put to our own use with skilful handling. She was a great subversive worker. Why should she not become the greatest of all 'treble' agents by working for us? He had struck the right chord. She jumped at it and I really believe she began to hate Bleicher from then on.

Her peculiar nature must have experienced a queer kind of elation at the idea of playing an even more complicated version of the game to which she had devoted herself. And perhaps the idea of personal revenge spurred her on.

By the time we had reached dessert, we were discussing what we should do. First came a bright idea. 'Well, Bleicher knows about us, but we also know about him now. We could trap and kill him!'

A half-smile appeared on Lucas' face and his eyes twinkled behind his glasses: 'Yes, of course, that could be arranged easily. Victoire could let you into their flat in the rue de la Faisanderie and when he comes home you could be waiting behind the door. But that wouldn't get us very far. He is not the only one who knows about us. Ah! yes, coffee, certainly, and three cognacs. They have some good stuff here.'

It was obvious that we could not simply bolt. That would have meant leaving our recruits stranded. My own fear was that I might have been trailed to various friends in my own circuit and that they would be in danger. This required verifying. In any case, London had to be warned as soon as possible about the wireless-transmitter. I told Lucas I wanted to meet Victoire again and question her to find out just where we stood. He agreed and said he would bring her along the next day.

He then leaned forward and said: 'I don't think the situation is hopeless. I have been forming a plan which could well turn the situation to our own advantage. As you will see, it all depends on Victoire, but I feel she can be trusted in this . . . now listen. . . .' And Lucas began to unfold his plan.

. . . . . .

I certainly had plenty to think of as I lay in bed that night. I had always laughed at the 'spy-thriller' type of story. I had never taken very seriously either the episode of the beautiful blonde countess who won the war by concealing the plans of the new secret aero-engine in her passion-rousing bosom, or that of the great battle of wits between the great Master-Minds of secret services, who played the future of mankind with men as pawns, on the chessboard of Europe. Yet here I was, in the midst of an intrigue straight out of a cheap edition, complete with beautiful blonde spy. Ours was neither blonde nor beautiful, but she would have to do. Our Master-Mind was some German called Bleicher who might not play chess, but who had at least got us beautifully taped. He knew where I lived, for instance; that was humiliating. Still, the overriding question was: had I been followed when seeing my own people? In vain I searched my memory for a suspicious incident. I had always taken every possible precaution, but you never knew. I could only find out by questioning the 'lady in the case' on the morrow. Why had we not been arrested already? She would probably also be able to explain that.

I went to the rendezvous the next day and found a calm, serious Lucas and an anxious Victoire. She was anxious because if I had disappeared suddenly her employers would have suspected an indiscretion and acted immediately. She relaxed when Lucas told her I had taken it well, and we got down to business.

She explained who Bleicher was, how he fitted into the counter-espionage business and how he worked. It was the chart on the blackboard all over again—the same names— Gestapo, Abwehr, Geheimefeldpolizei, Sicherheitsdienst, etc. I gathered that he was a Wehrmacht agent, not a member of the Gestapo. He enjoyed a great deal of independence and could conduct his investigations and actions very much as he liked and easily get all the backing he needed from his superiors and all sections of the Armed Forces. He had been left in charge of the exploitation of the capture of the Polish group—Victoire's betrayal had landed a fine catch—and now we were right in his clutches.

Why had we not been arrested already? Because a better idea was to let us build up a big group and then take everybody at once. Premature arrests would only yield our few miserable selves, new agents would doubtless be sent from London and Bleicher might not have the same luck in picking them up so quickly.

The ideal of counter-espionage was to let a subversive organization develop and even 'assist' by introducing some of their own people as recruits. Thus they could get to know all about British intentions and actually receive agents and supplies and, of course, discreetly prevent any of the targets being sabotaged. Then, when they thought things had gone far enough and that they had found out everything, they could arrest the lot in one big swoop. Victoire also said that another advantage of penetration was that the double agents and their German masters could get for themselves a large proportion of the money which London might send while the organization was still alive! They were in no hurry to kill the goose with the golden eggs.

This led to my big question: To what extent had I been

trailed? She said: Most probably not at all. They thought a man on the alert could easily detect followers, especially if he took routine precautions, such as making useless circles around blocks of buildings, and waiting to jump out of Metro trains until the doors were closing, when the 'shadow' would be faced with the choice of staying on the train and being whisked off or giving himself away by also jumping out hurriedly. (I had, in fact, been frequently doing these things and had noticed nothing suspicious.) The only efficient way of trailing a man through a big town was by using teams, the members of which could each keep him in view for a short time only and signal his movements to each other. This is more complicated than it sounds. No, Bleicher preferred to know certain places where we could be picked up, while Victoire was responsible for keeping Lucas and myself in sight by frequent meetings in bars and restaurants on which she had to report. At some of these, one of Bleicher's men would look on to check that we were 'all present and correct'. In any case the Germans had put me down as one of Lucas' junior lieutenants and had not realized that I was functionally quite independent. For this reason they had not bothered to find out whether I had any recruits of my own or not.

She emphasized that all this was based on Bleicher's trusting her to play her rôle. This was a risk he was willing to take. But, should there be any doubt created by an unexpected move on the part of one of us, the game would be up for the others, and in particular for her. As for my own case, she told me something personally interesting. I was the only member of the gang who was 100-per-cent British. Bleicher 'liked' the French and detested the British. When the time came to reap the harvest, 'honourable treatment' might possibly be granted to the others, but he would see that I was shot out of hand, as a pig-headed English swine!

The vital question was then examined: What were we to do? Here Lucas repeated his great plan, which we had agreed to submit to Victoire. So the Germans were counting on a big haul? Well, we would give them the promise of a success that exceeded their wildest dreams. Victoire was to report to Bleicher that Lucas had finally confided that he had been sent to organize a meeting, in Paris, of the main leaders of the circuits already in existence. They were far more numerous, far more active than the Germans had imagined. As 'chief attraction' of this imaginary conference, a British general was scheduled to arrive in France, to spend a day or so giving personal directives on co-ordination, after which he was to return to London to deliver his report. Lucas was to go to England to prepare the general's trip; he would leave by the M.T.B. scheduled to arrive on February 12th. Victoire would then suggest an extraordinary move: she would persuade Lucas to take her to England with him. On their return she could supply the Germans with top military information. What a master stroke that would be! A female agent going to London, sitting in on Secret Service meetings and drawing a British general into a trap, thereby smashing the entire Resistance movement! This was the fantastic plan we would dangle before the eyes of the Abwehr. Our own plan—the real one—was slightly different, of course.

Lucas and I planned to go with Victoire to meet the M.T.B. on the coast. As soon as the boat containing the two new agents reached shore, we would send them back on board, following with Victoire. We would all get back to England. When we got to London we would warn H.Q. that the Polish wireless had fallen into enemy hands. Victoire would tell the British everything she knew about German counter-espionage and the British, in turn, would immediately start sending a mass of false information via Radio-Bleicher. The possibilities seemed boundless, and were certainly worth the risk we ran in trying to outwit the enemy.

Once arrangements for use of the famous wireless-transmitter had been made, Lucas and I would secretly return to France to continue our missions, while Bleicher and his gang would begin to find the English general rather slow in coming.

This was Lucas' Machiavellian scheme for turning the tables on the Germans. I must admit it seemed quite a whopper to me. Victoire listened attentively without interrupting him a single time and, when he had finished, said it was very good, and she thought the Germans would buy it! Well, the only thing to do was to try and see what happened.

After this meeting I cautiously made a thorough security check of my own contacts. Everything seemed to be in order and I instructed my friends to 'go to sleep' for the time being and await my return. I made it clear that I would not send any unknown messengers. Lucas, Victoire and myself were to meet frequently to follow the development of the scheme.

At our next meeting Victoire was radiant. The Germans had swallowed the whole thing and were licking their chops in anticipation of the glorious catch. Lucas settled one or two details for Victoire's next report to the enemy. She was to tell them that she and Lucas would go to the coast to embark, and take me with them to meet the two agents who would be landing and escort them back to Paris. As I have already indicated our real plan was that all five of us go aboard, leaving no one on the beach. As soon as we reached London, we would send a message for Roger over the Victoire-Bleicher channel, worded as follows: 'For Roger Stop Arrived Safely Stop Regret Benoît and two Agents Embarked with Us Account Suspicious Movements on Beach Suggesting Discovery and Ambush. . . .'

This would sound quite plausible as the Germans were sure to have observers posted at the beach. It was amusing to think that the latter would most probably be reprimanded for having been clumsy enough to be spotted, thus alarming Benoît (myself).

I must, at this point, explain the particularly dangerous part Roger had accepted. Lucas had asked him to stay on in Paris. Bleicher would believe he was acting as 'locum tenens' until Lucas returned from London and have messages handed to him. His presence would help to dispel any suspicion that we might know the truth. He was to carry on as usual during all the time London would use the radio-link to deceive the enemy, then vanish when the order to do so was given through another channel.

I was inclined to be incredulous when I heard how the Germans had fallen for such a trick. Nevertheless, I believed Victoire's report. Could the enemy be such mugs? They had so far prepared and conducted the war intelligently. On a smaller scale, this Bleicher had soon found us out by means of his lady traitor and they were fooling London with the W/T set. What was there behind it all? Suddenly, the answer came in a flash. . . . Lies! That was it. . . . Lies! Lies and liars! These counter-espionage agents were themselves dealers in lies, and professional deceivers. Now, people who tell lies have a tendency to believe lies. I had observed this before. They seem to develop a queer mental kink. They are accustomed to make others serve their purposes by uttering words which have no foundation in truth or fact.

To them words seem to be the source of power. When words are spoken to them they are unconsciously impressed and their own conceit prevents their thinking that anyone would dare to try and deceive *them*! After all, we see many examples of this: shady big-business men who are taken in by the most ridiculous get-rich-quick schemes, great lawyers who are fooled by the most preposterous stories, politicians whose memoirs are sulky re-criminations about how they were easily bamboozled into signing away their country's best interests, etc. It was also a principle of Hitler's propagandists, that 'the bigger the lie, the more readily it will be believed'! Well, here was a very big one for Bleicher and Co.

As the date approached, other details were settled on both sides. Victoire informed us that Bleicher had arranged with the headquarters at Brest that the coast patrols would be kept in barracks at the beach to give us a clear field and that the M.T.B. was to be granted unhampered passage in and out. This was becoming really funny. That M.T.B. sneaking inshore on a moonless night with guns loaded and her crew at action stations would in fact be the only perfectly safe vessel in the whole of Europe! She could have a complimentary escort of Messerschmitts if we wanted! Bleicher had also made a little decision about me. As soon as Victoire and Lucas had left he would have me arrested with the two newly arrived agents. This should not upset the deception, as he would let Roger receive the news that I had been picked up by a routine coastguard patrol, which would have been quite likely if the operation had been a 'normal' one.

All this 'they don't know that we know that they know that we know that... etc.,' was enough to drive one crazy. I was glad that Lucas was handling it. I placed my trust in him absolutely and never doubted his cleverness and resolution. He was in command. On one point I put my foot down. While we would use the beach at Moulin-de-la-Rive, of which my friends had told me, I would not drag the local contact into it. The Germans must never know anything about him. There would be no safe house and no motor-lorry. We should walk and, if necessary, sleep under the stars (or even the rain).

During our several meetings Victoire reported to us a great deal of what the Germans were saying and thinking. She accompanied Bleicher when he met other Germans, including the Gestapo officers, with whom, of course, he was in contact. She said that at the time (January 1942) the opinion of the Gestapo was that the chances of Germany winning the war were fifty-fifty. In answer to her equivalent of, 'Tut, tut, gentlemen, are we not being a little pessimistic in view of our consistent military successes and the sweeping Japanese victories in the Far East?' the reply was: 'No, those damned English swine have managed to keep their communications open with the rest of the world, whereas we are properly boxed in.'

One day I could not go to lunch with Victoire and Lucas as arranged. I met Lucas in the afternoon, however, and he said she had been greatly perturbed. Had I cleared out? Didn't I trust her after all? If not, the whole scheme would collapse and she would lose her life. We hastened to meet her again so that I could re-assure her. She looked really anxious. When I told her my absence had nothing to do with any distrust, she calmed down and said I should not frighten her like that.

She told us that Bleicher had, of course, reported his plans to headquarters and that the Gestapo had found this scheme too clever to be feasible and were pressing for our immediate arrest. A big noise had arrived from Berlin to decide between the two proposals! Our only course was to still carry on as if we knew nothing and hope that Bleicher would win and the big shot decide in favour of our huge bluff. We were really in a lovely situation! The strange thing was that we did not seem to feel really jittery. Human nature is truly an incomprehensible thing. It may have been that we were so infuriated at having been found out that we wanted to beat them at their own game.

I was seeing quite a bit of Roger. He was great fun to be with, and his sense of humour was often stimulated by our strange situation. Every time we happened on a road-block, we would turn solemnly to each other and say: 'We're under observation by the Abwehr, after all. If these fellows try to pick a quarrel, we'll complain to the Gestapo, so there!'

During the few days remaining before the attempt, while Roger was getting ready for his lonely, dangerous rôle, we had drinks on the Champs-Elysées, lunch at the Tour d'Argent and an evening in a Montparnasse night-club.

After all, our position was rather comical. It was very funny to be able to know just what the enemy were thinking and practically have instructions given to them about the forthcoming operation. For instance, Victoire had told them that she, Lucas and I would go by train to Plouigneau and march from there to the beach at Moulin-de-la-Rive and that she would be wearing a red hat. I can imagine the ponderous German military order instructing all ranks to offer no hindrance to a trio including a woman with a red hat!

Finally the day came. On the evening of February 11th I boarded the Brest night express at Gare Montparnasse. Lucas and Victoire went to the station separately and entered another part of the train. This was to convince any spies that Lucas and I were still practising the security measures recommended in secret activities and did not know of their uselessness in this case.

When the train started I realized that I was beginning the craziest journey I should probably ever make. I dozed and nodded until the early hours of the morning when I alighted at Guingamp. I met my companions at the buffet. During the long wait for the local train we had coffee. Victoire had brought some real sugar and sandwiches. She was wearing the famous red hat.

We boarded the local stopping train for Plouigneau, this time together. Dawn broke during this part of the journey. The three of us had a compartment to ourselves until, at one of the stops, it was entered by three German N.C.O.s wearing Security Corps badges. As soon as the train re-started they turned to us and asked politely whether this *was* the train to Guingamp. We said no, we were actually going in the opposite direction. The Germans looked embarrassed and assumed wry grins, as they said how stupid they had been. They must have waited on the wrong platform. At the next stop our Feldwebels got out with many thanks for our information and apologies for having disturbed us.

As soon as they were gone we rolled about on the seats with laughter. We could just imagine these security N.C.O.s, having been ordered to check on our movements without alerting us, going to phone back a report on our passage with the assurance that all was in order and that we had not suspected anything! Lucas had a twinkle in his eye as he saw me come to realize that our opponents *could* be rather simple-minded.

We alighted at Plouigneau and set off on our march to the coast. The first village we headed for was called Lanmeur. We were enjoying the walk. It was not cold here and, as we were no longer surrounded by the walls and streets of a city, we were able to talk naturally as we swung along the country lanes, breathing the sweet, fragrant, morning air. There was nobody about and we could not be overheard. We chattered away about our extraordinary position, of course. We had begun to use certain words which were to enter the vocabulary of secret agents. These were: 'contaminated' and 'sick'. These expressions came naturally to us. A person who was under 'surveillance' by the enemy was 'contaminated'. He was at liberty and normal in appearance and might not be aware of having been spotted. Yet he was not only in grave danger himself but, like the carrier of a dreaded microbe, could contaminate others. This analogy with a contagious disease

F

was simply sensed by us, but it awaited the genius of a great writer for full expression. It was several years after the war that I read *La Peste* by Albert Camus. In this book the author conveys the atmosphere of the German occupation by transposing it into an imaginary epidemic of plague in an isolated city. It is an excellent illustration of our own situation at that time. The connection was, of course, the invisibility of the danger until it was too late, and all of us worried about carrying a disease which spared us temporarily only. In our present position we had been left apparently immune, so that we could, as the Germans thought, carry a lady-virus to London to fool the doctors into prescribing the wrong medicine, which would cause the disease to thrive instead of killing it. Luckily our enemies did not suspect that Dr. Lucas had isolated the germ into a test-tube and that it would be used to find the correct antidote.

As we approached Lanmeur we saw a uniform or two and guessed that they would be going to phone their report. They seemed to be stubbornly ignoring us. They could also have reported that we seemed to be very amused about something.

The two hours' walk to Lanmeur had made us quite hungry and we looked around for a restaurant. There was a small hotel and we went there. While we were eating, two French gendarmes came in and asked to see our papers. They asked us whether we had permits to be in the forbidden coastal zone. We 'confusedly' admitted that we had none, that we did not know they were necessary for this area (the usual excuse). The gendarmes took down our names and addresses. I remember they even asked for our mothers' maiden names and I had to think of one. They said we would be fined. We tried to look sheepish and ashamed. When they were gone Victoire explained in an undertone that friend Bleicher had obviously staged this incident, to prevent Lucas and myself feeling suspicious at being allowed to move freely in the coastal area.

After lunch we proceeded on our journey, and arrived at Moulin-de-la-Rive in the afternoon. It was in a small bay with some rocks. There were a few houses and a building obviously used as a barracks by the Germans. There were a number of guards about, but they took not the slightest notice of us. The sea was calm as a mill-pond. After a turn on the breakwater we sauntered on to Loquirec, where the houses were more numerous, and found an hotel. We asked if we could have dinner there. The manager did not seem very keen, but took us into the dining-room and served us with a good meal as we watched a magnificent sunset.

Since we had to pretend we were observing the curfew, we set out, a few minutes before ten, to return to the beach. On the road we saw the dark forms of two Germans in uniform. As we passed them they drifted to the other side of the road and turned their backs on us! My amazement grew. They must have known that Lucas and I were British officers, and, although our military record up to date may have given them a poor idea of our intelligence, they might have credited us with a few dregs of common sense. But no . . . they thought it quite plausible that we found it natural to be able to proceed along a coastal road at night without being challenged!

We fumbled our way on to the beach and lay down behind a pile of stones on the shingle. It was a long wait until midnight and we huddled together for warmth. Lucas whispered that he thought he detected a couple of figures crawling about near us. They must have been the observers from the Wehrmacht. I hoped they were feeling as cold as we were.

London's instructions (which had been faithfully relayed to us by the enemy) were that from midnight onwards we were to point a torch-lamp straight out to sea and flash a certain signal at regular intervals. When we saw the first arrival land on the beach, we were to exchange passwords and make ourselves known to each other.

At midnight I stood up, took the lamp and began to flash the signal. . . . The tide was coming in. The long wait had accustomed my eyes to the blackness and I could see dimly by that 'faint luminosity which fills the darkest nights'. I remember realizing that we were entering Friday the 13th of February. At the same instant a gold pencil-case I had been given as a parting gift in London fell from my pocket among the stones and I could not find it again. Was this a bad omen?

I kept flashing away and, after about half an hour, was beginning to wonder whether beach landings were as unreliable as dropping operations when I thought I saw a black form by the water's edge. I went forward and, sure enough, there was a man in gumboots walking along the beach.

He stopped as he saw me approach. I whispered the first half of the password and he answered with the second half. He said the M.T.B. was anchored out in the bay and that he had been put ashore in a boat further along the beach. The boat had returned to the M.T.B. to fetch the other agent and the equipment. Lucas and Victoire came up and we waited. The water which was lapping at our feet seemed to be getting slightly rough as the tide came in. After a while a black shape became visible. It was a very small boat rowed by a seaman. There was also another man in it. The sea had become quite choppy and the tiny craft was bobbing up and down. As it neared the beach a second boat appeared, also rowed by a seaman and with a passenger.

We waded into the surf to secure the boats and found that the waves were quite high. The passengers got out of the boats and floundered ashore. One of them was obviously the second agent, the other a naval officer in R.N. uniform, who introduced himself as the second-in-command of the M.T.B.

We explained that there must be a change in the plans and that everybody including ourselves must get back to the M.T.B. We tried to clamber into the boats but the waves came in higher and higher, and first one, then the other, craft was swamped and the seamen fell out. In an instant we were all in the water being buffeted by the breakers. I have never seen a storm blow up so suddenly.

The two seamen, the R.N. officer, the two agents, Lucas, Victoire and myself were helping to turn the boats upside down to pour the water out and then right them again. All the luggage the agents had brought fell into the sea. The boats proved to be absurd little things (I believe they are called pram-dinghies) and about as seaworthy as an inverted umbrella.

By now the sea was crashing on the beach and we could see five lines of surf gleaming white in the gloom. It was going to be impossible for anyone to climb aboard the flimsy boats. Also the oars had gone adrift.

It was quite an impressive spectacle. A short while ago the beach had been deserted and the silence of the moonless night broken only by the gentle lapping of the water's edge and now the darkness was agitated by eight people struggling in the foam and the roaring and pounding of the breakers. It was like battling against the powers of darkness.

The R.N. officer had a small flashlamp with which he was sending a long signal towards the invisible M.T.B. The struggle must have been going on for over an hour when the two seamen managed to push one of the overturned dinghies out through the surf and start swimming, using it as a float.

Some time later we discerned a large black shape being tossed up and down. I waded into the water again towards it and could see that it was a full-sized rowing-boat pointing towards the beach. I pushed on until the waves reached my shoulders and lifted me off my feet. The large boat was about thirty feet away, pitching madly, its bows towering above me. The crew were handling it with amazing skill, holding it stern to the waves, but could obviously come no nearer to the water's edge without getting into the breakers and foundering.

I gave up trying to reach it, swam and waded back to the beach and joined the others. The R.N. officer said it was the 'dinghy' or lifeboat from the M.T.B. I said it was a pity they had not used this 'real' boat in the first place. It would certainly not have capsized at the approach of a storm. Apparently this was blasphemy! The lifeboat was only supposed to be launched if the M.T.B. itself was sinking and the regulations must have been stretched a point for it to have put out for operational purposes. We watched the black shape jumping up and down on the wild waters for quite a time until it backed away and vanished into the noisy night.

It was all over. The M.T.B. would have to leave now in order to be out of sight of land before dawn. We gathered together. The two ratings had gone; there were six of us left on the beach.

Lucas decided that the two agents and the R.N. officer should hide in the woods and that the old trio should stay in the neighbourhood, so that Victoire could contact the Germans first thing in the morning, and that all six should meet again at the same spot the next night in the hope that the M.T.B. would return. Lucas' nimble brain had already devised another cock-and-bull story for Victoire to tell our Teutonic spectators, and a very plausible one it would sound. They had been able to see for themselves that the boat had come and that the storm had ruined the operation. The attempt would be repeated the following night and this time Lucas and Victoire would probably get away. Naturally, Benoît had to stay to help and the two agents would have to wait in hiding for Benoît. The sixth person, the R.N. officer, would also try to get aboard again. (If we had all six stayed together, and the two agents and the officer made no pretence of hiding, it would have been too obvious that we knew the truth.)

So the two groups parted and we three made our way back to Loquirec. The hotel was closed, and the people would not be roused. We sat in the yard until daybreak.

I was wet to the skin but could not remove my water-logged clothing.

When morning came we walked back to Moulin-de-la-Rive. The storm had subsided as the tide went out. Lucas and I entered a small café while Victoire went to the barracks to try to sell her story to the Germans.

After a while a Feldwebel entered the café and sat down. He passed the time of day in French with the serving-girl and then turned towards us and started a conversation. He had evidently been detailed to watch us while Victoire was away. He said he was tired of the war. He showed us photographs of his wife in Germany. There, at home, he had a motor-car, but here he could only ride a bicycle, etc. We made sympathetic noises and bought him a beer. He was most grateful and we were chatting pleasantly when Victoire came in. Our Feldwebel then departed with much smiling and saluting.

The three of us left the café and went for a walk while Victoire made her report. She had just seen the security officer in charge of the operation and told him she had left us at the café on a pretext that she wanted to buy some food from a farm and that she thought a woman alone would be more successful. The Germans had watched the catastrophic operation and were quite thrilled. They were very keen on a second attempt. They had, however, taken prisoner the R.N. officer. When Victoire had remonstrated with them, they had explained that he had not taken cover. They found him wandering in the open and had no option but to arrest him as he was in uniform. If they had not, Lucas and Benoît might have become suspicious! Victoire had said, yes, of course, she could see their point. They did not know where the two other agents had hidden. That was good news. Their luggage had been uncovered at low tide. One of the suitcases contained a wireless-transmitter.

The same arrangement with regard to confining the guards to barracks would be in force again for the next night, and they hoped the weather would be kinder.

We spent the rest of the day touring the villages of the area. My clothes were still very damp, but I hardly suffered from it. On the roads we would occasionally pass the now-familiar couple of N.C.O.s or officers looking the other way! We soon grew to take no more notice of them than policemen on point-duty! When night came we trudged back to the beach and flopped down for another vigil.

At midnight I started flashing the lamp, but nothing appeared, nor did the two agents come to the rendezvous. We still did not know what had become of them. We waited and waited, but nothing, absolutely nothing, happened. The sea was calm all through the night. We left, chilled and exhausted, in the early hours of the morning.

We made our way to Lanmeur and boarded a motor-bus for Morlaix. A German N.C.O. got in also and it was obvious from his 'appearing not to look like one', that he was our 'shadow'. At Morlaix we went to the station.

While waiting for a train we bought the papers, and read that the German battle-cruisers *Scharnhorst* and *Gneisenau* and the heavy cruiser *Prinz Eugen* had escaped from Brest, steamed up the Channel and only been engaged when they were in the Straits of Dover. They had got through without a scratch. This had happened on the 12th of February. Our own little catastrophe paled into insignificance. The British dispositions for interception must have proved as unsuitable in that major operation as the tiny cockle-shell pram-dinghies which had failed us in our little show. The news also set me thinking that the German counter-espionage officers must be very powerful indeed if they could have the coast patrols taken off at a time when the German Admiralty were busy scheming such a great operation *only a few miles away* at Brest and the entire coast must have been under strict security.

Lucas had made another plan. As things had gone wrong; the Germans might give the business up as a bad job and arrest us at any time. Therefore an alternative means of warning London must be found in case the main scheme fell through. He and Victoire would proceed to Paris and try to get a W/T message sent asking for another attempt to pick them up by sea, whilst I should break away from them and try to reach England under my own steam. He asked me to go through the unoccupied zone and contact his brother who might be able to help. If each of us succeeded, all the better. If only one succeeded, the purpose would be achieved. If both failed, we would have done our best.

We boarded the Paris express and I was able to relax for a few hours on the cushions of a first-class compartment in spite of my damp and faded clothing. Instead of going all the way to Paris, however, we got off at Le Mans. Victoire immediately went to find the field security officer and explained that Lucas wanted to contact some of his recruits there. That would seem quite natural; Bleicher knew his circuit had connections in the Sarthe region. I believe she also got Bleicher on the phone and confirmed that we were on our way back to Paris, so that he would maintain the existing arrangements. We went to different hotels and tried to rest.

The next day, instead of proceeding to Paris with them, I took a train to Tours. This was the critical moment. How would our followers react? We had so far acted on the principle that we were safe (!) so long as the three of us stayed together, but that I might well be arrested if it could be done without arousing Lucas' suspicions.

I was alone in the compartment until the train started. Just then a civilian got in with me. He asked if this was the train for Tours and made several clumsy efforts to start a conversation. He was obviously my shadow and sounded like a Frenchman. I decided I was safe until Tours. When we arrived there, in the evening, I saw a crowd of people milling around the German station-guard office. There was a punitive early curfew in force and arrivals had to queue up to obtain permits to leave the station and go through the streets. This was just the thing. I entered the rear of the crowd and wormed my way out through the side. I then gained the station entrance. My shadow had disappeared. I went to the booking-office and took a ticket to Bordeaux. There was an express due to leave shortly. I slipped into it and kept a look-out through the window. I had seen nothing suspicious by the time we started. Of course, I might have been watched at the booking-office and the clerk asked where I was going. This would not have mattered as I did not intend to go to Bordeaux at all. I kept awake and alert all night and got out at Angoulême. There I later caught a stopping train and alighted at Montmoreau. I had decided to get into the unoccupied zone by the pathway to Ribérac which I had used once before in the opposite direction.

Of course, the 'tame' locomotive from Bordeaux would have been better, but it was so good I wanted to save it for future use, and as I could not be quite sure that I was not still being trailed I did not want to risk leading the Germans to my excellent railway friends. Contaminating my friends had become an obsession.

At Montmoreau I found the small bus and travelled in it to the last village before the demarcation line. When we arrived there I marched swiftly along the road. At one point I saw two German officers walking slowly ahead. I slipped into a field and dashed for the path which led up the hill with the farm on top. I sped through the farmyard, was again barked at by the dog, raced down the other side of the hill and flung myself over the fence into the unoccupied zone. I hurried up the path and when the houses of Ribérac came into view I lit a glorious cigarette.

Of course, I had no guarantee that the Germans could not reach out into the free zone, but it would be infinitely easier for me to spot their spies. I took a bus to Périgueux and arrived there early in the afternoon. I had not thought much about food for several days, so I went to the station buffet. I was too late for lunch, but spotted some tins of foie gras on the counter. I ordered one of these and as it was very cold I also called for a bottle of wine and ate and drank the lot. When I got into the train I was shivering. The compartment was unheated. I believe the regulation was that the steam should only be turned on if the temperature fell below +7°C. (45°F.) and it was just about as cold as this. I got the only result which could be expected from the combination of the foie gras, the Chambertin and the chill: fantastic stomach-ache. Not the usual series of painful spasms, but the dreadful feeling of being crushed under a rock which had come to stay for ever.

My goal was Limoges, near which town Gauthier, Lucas' elder brother, lived. I arrived in the evening and tried to find a room in an hotel. I was told they were full. Late at night I finally entered a large establishment. There, to my great surprise, I was offered a very nice room. I flopped down and tried to recuperate.

Next morning I went to see Gauthier, whom I had informed by telephone of my arrival. As a precaution we met on the platform of a small country station about twenty kilometres from

Limoges. It was an interesting conversation with an interesting man. He was one of the very first local recruits of our organization. Lucas had enlisted his two brothers almost as soon as he dropped and Gauthier had already done quite a number of things. He had helped most of our agents who had arrived up to date in the unoccupied zone. He owned a large estate near Limoges, had seven children, seemed utterly fearless. He had been educated in England. His sense of humour was contagious. He asked me where I had spent the night. When I told him the name of the hotel in Limoges, and stated that I had been lucky to get a room there as all the other places were full, he explained that I had picked precisely the hotel occupied by the German delegations! With a twinkle in his eye he added that I had probably been safer in the lions' den than anywhere else, as the police would not have thought of looking for me there. It must have been my sure instinct which had led me to it. I said, no, it was a belly-ache.

He was extremely helpful. He advised me to go first to Vichy (the seat of the Pétain Government) and try to send a signal to London through a man he knew, who might be able to pass on a secret message. I could then proceed to Lyons to meet a lady who might be able to give me a contact for escaping out of France.

I returned to Limoges, took a ticket for Vichy and boarded the Lyons express that evening. Generally there was a change of trains at Saint-Germain-des Fossés. I was dead tired and all the seats were taken. I spoke to the attendant and he said he could fix me up with a *couchette*, a sleeping berth! A government official, for whom a berth had been reserved, had not turned up, so I could have it. As I lay down and loosened my sea-water-stiffened clothing, I offered up a silent '*Vive le Maréchal!*'

Our carriage was uncoupled from the express at Saint-Germain-des-Fossés and added to a local train which ran between there and Vichy. During this section of the journey, police-inspectors came around to check all identity papers. I behaved like the other three men in my compartment—snored, snorted, rolled over, fumbled for my wallet, clumsily spilled out the contents swore, yawned noisily and grumpily showed my identity card.

The police glanced cursorily at it, and withdrew, gently closing the door.

It is only a short run from Saint-Germain-des-Fossés to Vichy and we were soon there.

It was a miserable, bitterly cold day.

I had a look round the town and then went to the address Gauthier had given me. It was the embassy of a neutral country. I was eyed blankly at first. I must have been a sight. My shoes were discoloured by the sea-water and in my crumpled coat and trousers I looked like a tramp. After a few minutes of conversation in English my contact seemed prepared to trust me. I asked him to send a message to London warning that the ex-Polish transmitter was in enemy hands, but that the motor-boat pick-up of Lucas could be effected without risk. He said he understood perfectly, would do his best to help, and assured me of absolute secrecy.

I told him I must now get back to England as H.Q. would be urgently wanting every confirmation of this unbelievable story.

Having thus quickly finished my business in Vichy, I was free for the rest of the day, as I was taking the night train to Lyons. I therefore went for a look round. The temporary capital of unoccupied France was teeming with Army officers. The French were allowed an army in this zone, and the Marshal seemed to have quite a military establishment. One could not push open the swing-door of a café without colliding with three or four colonels. The various ministries had taken up their quarters in a number of hotels and people were hurrying in and out of the doors with papers and brief-cases.

I saw a detachment of soldiers lined up on the pavement in front of a small park opposite an hotel for some ceremony or other. People who had left their bicycles propped up against the railings were pushing their way among the soldiers and wheeling their machines out through the ranks while the ceremonial drill was in progress. I was astounded by the variety of uniforms in the streets. Many civilians were wearing the 'Francisque' on their lapels, the neo-Fascist-looking badge of the 'New Order'.

I went into a restaurant for some lunch and it was the most miserable meal I ever had. The portions were exactly the size prescribed by law and the waitress even demanded coupons for vegetables. I had never heard of this before.

Vichy was truly the comic-opera setting of officialdom wallowing in mediocrity. When they could no longer govern a great, historic nation, the bureaucrats were revelling in an orgy of petty regulations, paper tyranny, intrigue and police spying. Plain-clothes police-inspectors abounded. One of them stared hard at me and began to follow. My discoloured shoes and bedraggled appearance had certainly aroused his suspicions. I walked along until I came to a large café on a corner with a door on each street. I went round the corner and entered the café through the side door. I stood at the bar and watched my follower through the large glass windows as he turned the corner, stopped, looked up and down the street and finally shrugged his shoulders and went away. As I had expected, he had not thought of looking *into* the café windows.

In the evening I returned to the station and booked for Lyons. While I sat shivering in the icy waiting-room police came to check identity cards but left without asking any questions. I spent yet another night in a train. The French railways had become my flophouse.

At Lyons I set out to find the lady Gauthier had told me of. I was surprised to find a tall, blonde, charming, capable American girl. Her code name was Marie. She told me how to contact an escape route. I was to go to Marseilles for this. She also introduced me to another recruit of our organization, Joseph, who took me home that evening. For the first time for a week I was able to have a bath and a real night's sleep in clean pyjamas.

8. Mountaineering

I was in Marseilles by the following evening and went to a café called 'Le Petit Poucet'. I had a bit of trouble gaining the confidence of the manager. He eventually softened and put me in contact with a gentleman who was also very suspicious.

I was taken to the gentleman's home and there quite a long conversation ensued before I was able to convince my host that I was not a police spy. Fortunately, my business had taken me to the Marseilles area before the war, so that I was able to give him some details on certain mutual acquaintances and his doubts subsided.

The personality of this gentleman and of his wife showed that this was a serious organization. They put me up for the night and next morning I left in a small party for Toulouse, the first stage of our journey.

After a few days in Toulouse we were taken over by a Spanish guide and proceeded by rail through Perpignan to Banyuls. We arrived there at dusk. On leaving the station we soon climbed up on to the railway embankment and followed the lines away from town. Our long ramble on foot had begun. The guide told us to drop to our knees and crawl as we passed over a bridge. We left the railway as soon as we reached the foothills, cut through a wood of cork-oak trees and began our climb.

At about three in the morning we halted in front of a small hut, so tiny and low-roofed that we could not stand up inside. We were told it was normally used as a pig-sty. It was very cold, but lack of tobacco was hardest to bear. We were squatting inside the sty trying hard to rest when a man came running up, out of breath. Our guide obviously knew him and they began talking in Spanish. He was another guide who was supposed to bring two more 'customers' to join our party as we crossed the frontier. They were to meet us at the pig-sty. Unfortunately, they had not been as lucky as ourselves, having been shot at by the frontier guards, and the guide had lost his clients in the skirmish.

At the first light of dawn we got up, stretched our legs, and moved off, delighted to leave the uncomfortable shelter. We climbed up and up amidst rocks and bushes, until noon. The sky was cloudy and the weather still cold. We were beginning to feel tired. We stopped to lunch in the wild grandeur of the Pyrenees and resumed our journey much refreshed.

One of my companions was a middle-aged English major with a remarkable military career. A veteran of the First World War, he had volunteered again for this one. His military prowess had cost him an eye and a bayonet thrust in the belly. The latter imposed a very strict diet and, as he was unable to digest the *saucisson* which formed our rations, before leaving Toulouse we had had to get him a bit of cold chicken. It was actually that bayonet thrust which had led to his being with us. After being captured during the retreat towards Dunkirk, he had been sent to Germany, but because of his punctured bowels had been classified as disabled. On this account he was chosen to join the group of seriously wounded British prisoners who were to have been exchanged for a number of Germans in October 1941.

It will be remembered that this exchange was to have been made via Boulogne. The ships were ready, and all preparations completed, even to the brass bands on either side of the Channel. Just then the British and Russians marched into Persia and took a number of German prisoners. Hitler demanded that those of his fellow-countrymen who were in British custody should not be handed over to the Soviets. His request was disregarded, and he immediately cancelled the agreement. The British wounded had already been transferred to a staging camp near Rouen in preparation for their return. The major told me that, on learning of the cancellation, the German camp commandant had burst into tears, saying that he had been a prisoner himself during the First World War and realized the dreadful disappointment his British prisoners must be feeling. Our friend tried to cheer him up but, instead of shedding tears in his turn, he immediately formed a plan to escape. This stay of several days in France was too good a chance to miss! He got busy with his preparations and escaped a few nights later, taking fifteen men with him. He had managed by a miracle to contact the escape circuit, as the black patch over his empty eye-socket was a conspicuous identification mark.

We discovered that we were both Lancashire men and that he happened to know my godfather. As we tramped upwards, he revealed that he was haunted by the thought that he might one day die in bed. Then he told me what was bothering him . . . he had killed eighty-one Germans in the First World War, but only fifteen in 1940, including the one who had bayoneted him. That made a total of ninety-six, four short of the century. He could not die like that, he wanted those four badly. But once he got back to England, they might not let him out again. Couldn't I, as a special agent, do something to help? Perhaps our organization could use him? What was the age limit for parachuting?

I could not help thinking: 'What a man! You are the real British Army. With a few thousand more like you, Winston will get his blooming victory, sure enough!'

The major was certainly a picturesque character. He was wearing a splendid gold wrist-watch which had its little story. In 1940 the infantrymen who captured him had stolen all his valuables before the routine search. The major, old Army man that he was, had managed to hide his wrist-watch by wrapping it cunningly around his virile attributes!

His memories of his military career poured forth as we continued our journey. He had volunteered to fight for King and Country in 1914, but what had he been given as a first assignment? Guard duty in the barracks W.C., with a big stick to wallop those who forgot to pull the chain! Of course he had later seen real action, but he was still short of those four. . . . He entertained us with his stories and complaints, so that we forgot our fatigue as we marched along.

The third 'client' of our group was a charming Polish R.A.F. pilot whose bomber had been shot down over Holland on that notorious winter night of 1941-2 when three dozen of our aircraft failed to return. He had baled out and broken a leg on landing. In spite of this he had succeeded in reaching Marseilles and the escape route.

The major had little use for the 'Flying Corps'. 'Oh, yes, we know the Air Force always arrive late. Never saw you in May 1940. And what about the *Scharnhorst* and the *Gneisenau*? The "Flying Corps" must have been in bed!'

The 'Flying Corps' would retort angrily: 'What about ze Battel of Britain—eet was weez your boots ze Heinkel and Messerschmitt was brought down—yes?'

I was well qualified to act as arbitrator, as I was technically a member of the P.B.I. and practically a passenger of the R.A.F.

The going was easier after we passed the summit and in the late afternoon reached the slopes on the Spanish side. When the first village came into view we halted and remained hidden until nightfall. The worst was over. We resumed our walk in the dark and at eleven o'clock that night reached the railway at Vilajuiga and hid again until it was time to take the early-morning train. Thanks to the splendid organization of the escape route, we arrived in Barcelona without having once been interfered with. As we left the station I was struck by what now seems an insignificant detail; our guide took us to a café where we were served milk; I had seen no milk in public for weeks. Then, trying not to look hurried, we went for a walk, sauntering, as if by chance, past the British Consulate. At a signal we suddenly slipped inside and out of the way of the Falangists.

I was immediately led into the Consul's office. He had just received instructions concerning me (Lucas and Victoire had succeeded in reaching London and had warned H.Q. that I was on my way). Arrangements would immediately be made to get me home quickly. Although there still remained some risks to be

G

taken, I was no longer a fugitive but a 'special agent', a mysterious 'de-luxe' animal entitled to consideration and top priority just like a V.I.P. Ah, that tin of Gold Flakes the Consul gave me!

The major and I continued our journey by car, leaving our Polish friend in Barcelona to be picked up by another 'convoy'. It was extremely hot in Madrid, but I caught a nasty cold nevertheless, and the major nursed me like a father. He had discovered, however, that I was only a lieutenant then, and if I turned up late for lunch in our 'private room' in the basement of the Embassy, he would greet me with a 'Good afternoon' as frigid as anything the most frightening C.O. could achieve in any mess.

I left the major in Madrid and was driven to the Portuguese frontier which I crossed during an exhausting march in the mud between Badajoz and Elvas, on the way to Lisbon. A few days later I was put aboard a plane at Cintra Airport. I had taken advantage of my stay in Portugal to fill a suitcase with butter, eggs, silk stockings, oranges, etc.—which articles were either rationed or unobtainable in England—to ensure my popularity on arrival! I was warmly welcomed when I arrived in London that same evening by two officers of the section.

The next morning I went to H.Q. and found Lucas. Victoire and he had returned to Paris when we had parted at Le Mans. She had explained my disappearance away to the Germans by saying that Lucas had told me to go south to try and find another way out for them in the event of the M.T.B. failing again. She said we had heard of a smugglers' boat operating on the Mediterranean coast. Perhaps I had been pinched by the Vichy police in Unoccupied France. If I had managed to lose my German shadowers, they must have been damned clumsy! The second M.T.B. operation had been arranged by Radio-Victoire at another spot on the Breton coast and this time was successful in a calm sea.

I was interviewed by a number of senior officers and others who were concerned with trying to use the extraordinary device which had been given to them—a radio-link with the enemy. I know that in later years our H.Q. had to deal with a number of 'played-back' transmitters, but it must have been a novelty then and it caused much excitement. A new euphemism was coined: when the enemy was operating one of your own sets, it was said to be 'controlled'.

My testimony was considered to be that of an independent witness and helped Headquarters to decide on the best course to follow. It was decided that Lucas was to return to Paris to resume work with his contacts while messages would be sent through the 'controlled' radio to give the impression that he was still in London with Victoire. He would actually be in touch with H.Q. through another operator who was being sent out.

I also learned that the two agents who had been landed at Moulin-de-la-Rive had been arrested at a farmhouse where they had sought shelter. That is why they had not turned up on the beach on the second night.

Lucas was due to be parachuted back into France during the next moon-period. I was to return during the following period to reactivate my own contacts. He left one evening and a few days later I was told he had dropped according to plan.

Then we had bad news. After seventeen days in Paris Lucas had been arrested. Roger and Gaston were also taken. Their bold plan had miscarried.

Looking back on those activities of our organization which had come to my knowledge so far, the balance-sheet appeared as follows: The casualty rate had been enormous. Almost all the men sent to France in 1941 had been wiped out. I myself had escaped only through the most extraordinary combination of circumstances. I had been unable to blow up any of my targets. The enemy had penetrated us. Our early equipment and means of communication had proved inadequate.

On the credit side, Lucas had caused the Germans to lose their precious Victoire and provided our own H.Q. with a means of counter-penetration. We had laid the foundation of a network which was to bear fruit later. We had also obtained a great deal of experience, which is said to be cheap at any price.

Conclusion of Part One

LUCAS, Roger, Gaston, Denis, Besnier, the two agents who landed in Brittany and a number of others were sent to captivity in Germany for the rest of the war.

Victoire was kept in England. The extent of the damage she had caused in the days following her arrest being known to the Allies, she was gradually 'cooled down', her movements were restricted more and more and she was finally put in jail, where she remained until the liberation of France, to be handed to the French, who wanted to call her to account for the part she had played between the time she was arrested by the Germans and the time she threw in her lot with us. She was tried in Paris and sentenced to death, but later reprieved.

Her case is an extraordinary and unsavoury one.

This woman had started by doing dangerous intelligence work for the Allies as soon as France was overrun and at a time when things looked hopeless. She had been arrested and, unable to endure imprisonment even for a few days, had purchased her liberty by betraying a great number of her comrades.

As I was not present at her trial, I do not know the extent of the crimes with which this strange, unbalanced woman was charged. I have heard that, on her own admission, she was responsible for the capture of sixty or seventy men, of whom about fifty were executed.

When, however, she did decide to turn against the Germans, she seems to have done so wholeheartedly in spite of the enormous risk involved, and at a time when the German star appeared, from inside occupied nations, to be still high in the heavens. Was she trying to work her passage home, or did she simply want to be the most fabulous of woman spies?

I have been told that during her trial she expressed no repentance, her attitude was boastful and she laughed when the death-sentence was passed.

I recall that when I arrived back in England and was discussing with an intelligence officer my experiences in this case and the possibilities it offered, he asked, 'Why do you think she did all this?' I replied: 'Because she liked it. She likes to feel she wields sinister power over men. Also, she might have been just a little fond of us.'

He asked, 'Do you think she intends to play the game with us?'

'Yes,' I replied, 'I think she has at the moment every intention of doing so, although I cannot predict what would happen if we sent her back to Paris.'

Such are my recollections of the villainess in whose company I had occasion to dine, wine, laugh, scheme, march and flounder in a rough sea.

I still think that Lucas handled the situation in the best possible way. When, after the war, it was learned that the Germans had, thanks to the playing-back of one of the first W/T sets, for a long period controlled all our Secret Service activities in Holland, I felt that his counter-penetration of the Abwehr may well have prevented a French 'North Pole'.

As for Herr Hugo Bleicher, whom I had never seen but heard so much of, I was to meet him by chance after the war in Paris. He had apparently remained very active for the rest of the occupation, had penetrated several of our circuits, caught a number of agents, played back several of our W/T transmitters and generally done a lot of damage to our organization. He had been caught during the retreat to Germany, held prisoner in England for a short time and handed over to the French, who were finally employing him to clear up a number of treason cases. We had both been called as witnesses in one of these and he was pointed out to me in the waiting-room. I went up to him and rather startled him by saying I was Benoît. He said: 'Ah! you escaped, but, you know, I have never beaten or hit anybody. I did not ill-treat Lucas nor any of your other friends. It was I who avoided their being shot . . . etc. . . . etc. . . .'

He then looked at me almost pleadingly, and suddenly asked, 'Tell me, I beg of you . . . La Chatte . . . is it true she was double-crossing me?' This proved beyond a doubt that our manœuvre had succeeded and that for once the Germans had been properly fooled.

PART TWO

9. Alexandre

ALEXANDRE and I were the only passengers in the vast central section of the Halifax. The two packages containing our luggage were lying on the floor, attached to their parachutes. Along the walls ran the ammunition-racks with the brass of their thousands of rounds shining like golden ribbons.

I had been in London for the last two months. For this second mission I had chosen to jump 'blind', as there had been so many casualties among our agents and the situation seemed so confused that I did not want to run the risk of being received by a contaminated committee. We were to be dropped in open country in the neighbourhood of Bellac and would find our way about when we reached the ground.

At the aerodrome it was obvious that we would be travelling in greater style than the first time. The machine was a four-engined Halifax bomber, which we had all to ourselves. For luggage we were allowed real suitcases which were to be dropped with us by separate parachutes. There was no arguing about pyjamas, also we had considerably more money.

The dispatcher was a Polish sergeant. His English was limited and he conversed with us by gestures and grins.

I was expecting the journey would again take three hours. When they had elapsed and there were no signs of preparation I asked for our position. The captain sent word over the intercom that we were near Le Havre. I reckoned this was only 200 miles from our starting-point. It seemed strange and I asked what our speed was. The dispatcher went to the cockpit to find out and came back to say we were flying at sixteen. I remembered that air-speed indicators were graduated in tens of miles per hour, so our speed was 160. We must have been circling quite a bit to lose a couple of hours. We were still far from the target and I began to doze.

Two hours later the dispatcher hurriedly raised the exit-hatch and pointed downwards. The red light came on and Alexandre had barely time to reach the edge before it turned to green. He dropped out into the dark, the sergeant threw a package after him and then I pushed off.

When the blast had subsided and I had stopped swinging, I thought I was at an altitude greater than normal. By the moonlight I spotted another parachute about a hundred yards away and fifty feet above and guessed that it was the second package.

I landed on a steep bank at the edge of a wood, twisting my right ankle. I saw the other 'chute land and went to collect it. After dragging it to the edge of the wood, I set off back along the line of flight but soon came to a bog. I risked flashing my torch and softly calling 'Alexandre'. There was no answer. I felt my way around the bog and searched for well over an hour with no result. I returned to my gear, opened the package, and was glad to find my own suitcase inside. As we were two hours late and the nights are short in May, there was not much time before dawn, so I dug a shallow hole with the small spade which was always provided in the leg of the flying-suit and buried the two 'chutes and all the rest of the equipment.

I was worried at the disappearance of my companion and resolved to make a thorough search at daybreak.

Alexandre was a British officer who had been given into my care. I was to set him up in business by introducing him to some of my contacts and guiding his first steps. His qualifications for this kind of work were like my own: he spoke French fluently and had grown weary of military spit-and-polish and English cooking. We had immediately become friends. We had of course provided for the event of our becoming separated on landing and fixed an emergency rendezvous in Tarbes, which was to be our first port of call, but I feared he might have crashed and been seriously injured or knocked out.

With the first light of dawn the birds began to stir . . . and I found I had landed a few hundred yards from a hamlet and still closer to a high-voltage overhead power line! I hid my suitcase in some bushes and set out to search the area. I spent the whole of the day scouring the fields and woods but found no trace of my friend. Moreover, I could not make out just where I was. I finally marched along a narrow lane and at last came to a main road and found a *borne kilométrique*. By comparing the markings thereon with my Michelin map, I worked out my location and discovered that we had been dropped sixty-five kilometres (forty miles) away from the agreed spot! I was at a point near Grand-Bourg, north-east of Limoges.

That afternoon I returned to where I had left my suitcase. The few country-people I saw stared at me but I was too concerned about Alexandre to worry. I stayed all the next night at the place where I had dropped in case Alexandre should also be searching for me. When dawn came again I decided he must have gone on his way, so I picked up my luggage and set out to march to the nearest railway station at Marsac, about seven miles away, according to my map. My ankle was painful and I limped along cursing the Halifax, its navigator, its pilot and each one of its four engines in turn.

I eventually found Alexandre a couple of days later drinking beer in a café at Tarbes. He had landed on the opposite side of the bog, had looked for me all night and left the morning after.

We first went to see Rechenmann, a recruit of mine whom I had made my agent in the unoccupied zone during my first trip. He was an Alsatian engineer posted in the free zone by the same firm for which my friend Nel worked. He was in communication with some of my friends in Paris. He said all was well and they were expecting my return. He also confirmed that the express locomotive was still running smoothly. So Alexandre and I set forth on our travels around the 'underworld'.

In London I had gathered that the situation could briefly be summed up as follows: After the bad mauling our organization had suffered in its beginnings in 1941, a number of new agents had been sent to each zone to replace the casualties, and were busy 'opening shop' in various parts of the country. There were not many in the field as yet, but the aim was to have a high proportion of radio-operators so that each organizer would eventually have his own.

Several operators had been sent recently to the free zone. During my briefing I had been told that one of these had been instructed to get in touch with the admirable Marie, who had 'shown me the way to go home'. I should go to see her and arrange for his going to Paris, where he would then work for Alexandre.

Our next objective was therefore Lyons. During our journey I began to coach my companion in elementary security. We stayed together in the trains, but on arrival parted on the platform, passed separately through the barrier with its contingents of plain-clothes and uniformed police, went to different hotels and met later at a prearranged rendezvous in town.

I was happy to find Marie and introduced Alexandre. She was charming and efficient and ready to give every assistance. She told us where our man was staying, so we decided to go there at once and begin preparations for his crossing the line and transporting his set.

We had a look around Lyons, which is a very big city. I have heard argument about which of Lyons or Marseilles is the largest city in France after Paris. As in other towns in the unoccupied zone there were a few motor-taxis, but one had to apply to a police station and give particulars in order to use one, so we took the famous rickety tramcars, which groaned and clattered along the streets.

The food situation was the same as in other large towns—plenty of everything (except fats and sugar) for the wealthy minority and habitual hunger for the others. Whenever I recall memories of the occupation, two tastes come to my mouth—those of the horrible acorn 'coffee' and of the beastly brown 'bread'. While men in my position could frequently obtain lavish meals, they had to travel a great deal and could not use the black market all the time, so I had my share of regulation food and know perfectly well how the majority of French people suffered from undernourishment.

We found our W/T operator, he was unable to go to the occupied zone immediately with us, and asked to be allowed to leave a few days later. He would join us in Paris. I took Alexandre to Montauban to initiate him in my way of crossing the demarcation line. We contacted sweet little Edwige, who warned the crew of the engine. As it was more difficult to get boxed *into* the cavity under the tender than to get out of it, we had to be put inside in the engine depot at Montauban and stay there all the way to Bordeaux. Thus, when going *into* the occupied zone, I could not play at being an engine-driver.

The two of us just about filled the space as we lay side by side and head to feet. As we dozed during the four-hour night journey, we frequently woke each other up by pushing our shoes into each other's face. Our luggage was concealed in various lockers somewhere else in the huge tender.

There was the usual fifty-minute search at Langon, the arrival at Bordeaux, the shunting from the train to the depot and finally, just as curfew ended in the early morning, we were in the street and walking sleepily towards the main station.

We spent the day in Bordeaux while Alexandre got his first look at the German Army. We also discovered a way of getting in and out of the main station without going through the ticket barrier. There was a door at the back of the hall of the station hotel which opened into the 'Wagon-Lits' office. This in turn was accessible from one of the platforms. We tried it both ways. These curious loopholes in the guarding were sometimes very useful. I was to find others in various stations.

We took the night express and arrived in Paris on a lovely spring morning. We went to register at different hotels as usual and later met, so that I could take Alexandre on our round of visits. After a few days he was busy chasing about organizing a circuit. My friends procured him a black-market bicycle. As we were inside Paris, it was necessary for him to go to the police station to register it and obtain a number, like a motor-car. He also had to state on oath that he was not a Jew.

H.Q. in London had not been too happy about my staying in Paris as the Victoire business must have put me on the 'wanted' list and it was pretty certain that several Germans knew me by sight and had probably photographed me. However, Paris is a big place and I was not particularly worried. Nevertheless, I avoided the bars and restaurants I had previously visited regularly.

The propaganda campaign for volunteers for the 'L.V.F.', which was fighting in Russia, was being somewhat intensified. Some of these recruits were to be met in Paris. They wore German uniforms but could be identified by a small tricolour flash. This was, however, not really necessary, as they generally looked dirty and sloppy. More than once I saw the smart German soldiers glancing at them with contemptuous expressions.

The invitations to go and work in Germany were becoming more pressing. Conscription of labour was not yet in force but, due to the heavy losses on the Russian front, the Nazis were evidently beginning to feel a shortage of manpower.

This melting of the enemy's manpower in the Russian crucible was a great source of encouragement to the French. It is true the Nazis were advancing swiftly towards the heart of that huge country, but it could only be at heavy cost.

By now part of the population had become aware that there might also be a secret war in progress, although they could not understand just what it consisted of. It should be explained that in France, during peace-time, all kinds of legends had been built up about the 'British Intelligence Service'. It had inspired much fiction and many espionage thrillers. It was supposed to be a vast esoteric, omniscient organization commanding unlimited means of action to further the interests of 'eternal England'. In particular, it had an unlimited supply of 'St. George's cavalry'. Few Frenchmen doubted that this wonderful institution was at work in its own mysterious way and that most of the unpleasant things which would happen to the enemy in the future could be traced by devious means to the long-term cunning of anonymous super-schemers, who worked somewhere in the Foreign Office and concealed their activities by appearing at fashionable Mayfair tea-parties wearing the most stupid expression on their faces and talking only about horse-riding, grouse shooting and memories of their days at Oxford or Cambridge. Later in the evening they would leave their exclusive clubs to go and study a report from a Captain 'X', who might be passing for a snake-charmer some-where in India, a moujik in Astrakhan, an innkeeper in Cologne or an abstract painter in Paris. They would also from force of habit send off a couple of million pounds to buy the conscience of some oriental pacha, in order to get a new oil-well for perfidious Albion and so to bed to dream up new Machiavellian plots.

It was therefore inevitable that, when I revealed myself to a French friend, I was automatically classed as a member of the 'Intelligence Service' and became clothed with an aura of traditional mystery. It was touching to see how their conviction blinded them to the obvious total lack of intelligence of any kind whatever which had led to the Munich agreement, the 'phoney war', the invasion of Norway, Dunkirk, and other weird 'strategic conceptions' which had distinguished our war-making up to date. Those events must have taken place while the Master-Minds were drinking their tea in Mayfair, but now Winston Churchill would alter all that, make them take tea in their offices and victory would soon come.

My own lack of weapons, explosives, money and know-how could only be a blind!

My fellow-agents had much the same experience and it is a fact that throughout the war and for years afterwards we were referred to as 'agents de l'Intelligence Service'. If I did try to explain that, had they been able to see me in London, I would have been wearing a regulation officer's uniform and that I was on a special but nevertheless military assignment, they would say, with a knowing air, 'Ah, yes—War Office.'

This designation 'War Office', in fact, later became practically official to distinguish 'F Section' agents, who were commanded directly by the British, from 'B.C.R.A.' agents who were controlled by the Free French Government-in-exile led by General de Gaulle.

The position was that General de Gaulle wanted to organize secret activities inside France and, quite understandably, to control them from his headquarters in London. Some French officers who had followed him there had volunteered and been trained in the British special schools and infiltrated into France with various missions—intelligence, sabotage, preparations for organizing and arming French patriots as guerillas against the day when the Allies should land, propaganda, political preparation for taking over the government of the country as soon as the as-yet-distant liberation should come, etc.

It was equally understandable that the British High Command, who were responsible for dealing with any Axis military activities anywhere, should also want some of their own special agents in France, which was the most important occupied country. The enemy forces in France constituted the most direct and immediate threat to Britain, and the most decisive actions of the war would have to be fought on French soil. The notorious disagreements in London had made unity of command impossible and there were thus two rival firms in the field. The British, of course, provided transportation, equipment and W/T reception facilities for the French B.C.R.A. but did not interfere with their operations. For their recruits the British had taken some members of the Services who spoke French well, such as myself, and also some Frenchmen who, having escaped from France and reached England, had been dissatisfied with their reception by the Free French Government-in-exile and preferred to serve with us.

This dispute in high quarters at home was regretted by agents in the field, but we kept it from our recruits. The excellent broadcasts in French on the B.B.C. with Maurice Schumann's nightly address stressed unity of purpose, and so long as anything came from London our friends were satisfied.

However, we began to 'run into each other'. One of my own men would tell me that a friend of his had joined another local resistance group, which was controlled by a leader who was in contact with an 'emissary from London'. I would explain that compartmentalization was necessary and that each man must follow his leader.

The B.C.R.A. were also having their troubles and suffering heavy casualties, as we had done.

To return to my own movements, I was keeping in touch with Alexandre until his W/T operator should arrive as arranged. He was soon overdue and we began to worry. I remember that the place of rendezvous I had specified was the most obvious feature of Paris: we were to meet under the Eiffel Tower!

The appointed hour was 1 p.m. every day and, in the lovely weather, it was quite natural that two men who looked like office clerks should relax there after lunch.

Speaking of lunch, I remember that one day I went alone to a new restaurant and noticed that certain of the clients were being served with good black-market food. I asked for some and was served without question. When I paid the bill I remarked to the manager that it was good of him to have trusted me. He replied that he had seen I was on my own and that, as the police always came in pairs, he knew I was all right.

The same evening Alexandre and I had dinner together in another restaurant we were visiting for the first time, and I again saw some diners being very well looked after. I again asked if we could not partake in their 'off-the-menu' dishes and we were again immediately served as requested.

While paying the bill I made the same remark and the manager replied that *he* knew we were safe enough as the police *never* came in pairs. Ah, well! thus did doctors disagree.

Our own experts could not be blindly trusted either. One evening I was in my hotel room making up a parcel of underwear to be sent to the laundry and I recalled that our H.Q. in London were particularly proud of their newly formed clothing department. They had claimed that they issued us only with special suits and underwear of French cut and that they even went to the trouble of procuring labels of French tailors and haberdashers to stitch on, such was the attention to detail. As I laid out my pyjamas I noticed the tag inside the collar of the jacket. It read: 'HARROD'S—THE MAN'S SHOP'!

When a certain number of days had elapsed without the operator appearing, it was decided that I had better go to Lyons to try to find out if anything was wrong. Once again my locomotive friends took me across inside the now-familiar tender.

In Lyons, Marie told me that the operator had failed to get across the demarcation line near Loches. He had not been arrested, but was being replaced by another, more resourceful, man, whose wireless-set was to be carried to Paris separately by a courier. I wanted to push the lot across in my locomotive, but everything was already laid on, and the arrangements were claimed to be very good, so off they went.

I had a number of things to do in the unoccupied zone for the next few days and I frequently passed through Lyons. I saw a lot of Marie and was very happy to do so. She was paying the price of having a strong, reliable personality: everybody brought their troubles to her, and our H.Q. in London sent their troubles in the form of agents who were told to contact her to find W/T operators! She was so willing to help that when a needy visitor came she would give her ration cards away, wash clothing and make contacts for him. She had even found out in which jails some of our unfortunate friends were held.

As there were now several W/T operators in the Lyons area, communication with H.Q. was ensured, supplies were being dropped and a few bangs were being made. The show was on.

At this time I was not resident in any particular area as my targets were widespread. I was again travelling a great deal. I sometimes had to carry small quantities of sabotage equipment for considerable distances.

One day, while in the unoccupied zone, I found a 'client' near Limoges. As the next moon-period was a couple of weeks away, I decided to take to him some stuff which I had received from a drop quite near Lyons. I packed eighty pounds of explosives, incendiaries, time-pencils, Sten-guns and ammunition into two large suitcases and set off for the station with my burden. I did not use a porter as I did not want the unusual weight to be noticed. I reached the station safely. I have already mentioned that there were sometimes curious loopholes in the security arrangements.

I had spotted one of these at this station: there was a left-luggage office which had two counters, one in the main booking-hall and another on the opposite side which lined the first platform. I therefore checked in my heavy suitcases in the hall and shrugged my shoulders when the clerk commented on their great weight, purchased my ticket, went through the well-guarded ticket barrier and withdrew them from the platform counter on the other side—telling the clerk that I had just learned that a train was leaving for my destination at once. The train was full, so this gave me an excuse for leaving my weighty suitcases in the corridor.

Inside the station was standing another train—and a horrible one. It was formed of large enclosed goods-waggons, the sliding doors of which were half open. On the ground opposite each door an armed and helmeted sentry was standing with his rifle. Through the doors could be seen part of the pitiful cargo—Jews apparently, chiefly women and children, trying to press their pale faces into the opening for a breath of air.

A nurse was walking along the six-foot way with a bucket of water, filling small tin cups and lifting them to the outstretched hands. A prisoner who had fainted was being taken through one of the open doors. Man or woman? I could not see. The poor wretched human being was placed on a stretcher carried by two ambulance men, and as they bore it away, began to vomit.

So it was happening here—this vision of Nazi-dominated eastern Europe was in the main station at Lyons in *Unoccupied* France. The miserable Vichy Government had not even thought it necessary to stop the train outside in the marshalling-yard. I was filled with rage—I thought of those Sten-guns in my bag. I wanted to yell out for half a dozen resolute men to mow down those

H

guards, but a fat lot of good it would have done—the poor wretches would never have been able to get out of the station. I swallowed my rage and resolved to play the worm, as a secret agent so often has to do.

I do not know where they were going; probably to be handed over to the Germans as a gesture of 'collaboration'.

When my own train started I was standing at the end of the corridor with a number of other passengers who had no seats. Near me was an old lady, so I folded my coat over the top of my bags and offered it to her as a seat. She sat down gratefully and said it was so kind of me to look after an old woman. Poor grandma, if she had only known she was sitting on enough stuff to blow the whole carriage to smithereens and that I had only thought her presence would discourage anyone from trying to move those suspiciously heavy bags out of the way, she would have been very disappointed. At Limoges I changed from the crowded express to a local train and alighted at a small country station. I toted my load along a narrow lane and there was my 'client' waiting—with a broad grin and—thank goodness—a wheelbarrow.

A couple of days later I returned to Lyons and called on Marie early in the morning. I was very sleepy. She gave me some breakfast and made me lie down on a couch to rest. As I dozed, I had a dream and then awoke completely and saw it was no dream —there were Alexandre and his W/T operator standing over me. I sat up, stared at them, and uttered the obvious remark, 'Why, I thought you were in Paris!'

Alexandre explained. The operator had been caught with a whole convoy of people while crossing the demarcation line. That damned line again! The wonderful passage which had been promised had proved a wash-out. They had walked straight into the arms of the German guards. However, our boy had not taken it lying down. After a few hours' detention, as the prisoners were being loaded into motor-trucks to be taken to jail, he made a dash for it and got away. He managed to reach Paris and met Alexandre at the rendezvous.

This was fine. All that was then needed was his transmitter which, as I have already stated, was being carried separately by a courier. They waited for several days until they decided that the courier had probably got into trouble also. This was too much for the dynamic, impatient Alexandre. Without a set, the W/T operator could not send messages to London for supplies and he knew of no alternative means of communication. (I could not help thinking he was also fortunate not to have met any obliging Victoires!)

The W/T operator said he knew of a spare set in Lyons but there was the vital matter of wavelengths, crystals, schedules, plans, etc., which would have to be arranged with London by an exchange of messages through a station already operating regularly in Lyons.

Alexandre was determined not to lose sight of his operator this time and so came with him, having made a vow that he would take back a complete outfit in working order—man, set, crystals and all. This had brought them to Marie's.

I asked how they had crossed the line. Alexandre paused before answering and then out came the big item—he had found a patent route of his own. He had been impressed by my steam locomotive, had determined to do better, and had found an *electric* locomotive! Yes, he had got in touch with the driver of the Paris–Toulouse express which crossed the line at Vierzon, and they had both been hidden inside the machinery. They had alighted at Limoges and could return by the same means. The electric engine was, of course, cleaner than the steam one and it had been more comfortable. Alexandre told me all this with the slightly nervous voice of the novice who has dared to go one better than the veteran! I warmly congratulated him. This was the right spirit. Do not keep relying on what others provide. Make your own contacts and arrangements and become independent as soon as possible. Here was a man with the makings of a great special agent. He was obsessed by the idea that the Allies might decide to invade the Continent that summer and that he would be late with his supporting demolitions. He wanted to become active. He said that if he could not fix up this wretched W/T business and get some explosives delivered, he would see red and try to smash up his targets with a jemmy and his finger-nails.

I pointed out there were very few signs of a landing in France in 1942 and he finally calmed down.

Within a few days the spare set had been found, the procedure fixed with H.Q., and the pair were ready to return to Paris.

Marie had just received a visit from several new agents who had been landed by boat on the Mediterranean coast. One of them was bound for the occupied zone. Could she give him a good tip for crossing the line? Alexandre said he would be happy to take him in his electric engine, and so the pair became a trio, and off they went to Limoges, the first stage of their journey. Alexandre was carrying the incriminating W/T set in his luggage as he had no more use for special couriers who got lost.

I resumed my travels and among other things, one night in the country, received a delivery of a few containers. In addition to the usual supplies, there was a small special parcel for Marie, so at the first opportunity I returned to Lyons to give it to her. When she opened the door in answer to my ring, she exclaimed: 'Thank God! You are a sight for sore eyes!'

She ushered me in and said she had been afraid I had also been arrested.

—Why also? Who has been arrested?

—Alexandre. . . .

—What? Alexandre?

—Yes, and the two others. . . .

A few days after the trio had left for Limoges and Paris, one of her remarkable grapevines had informed her that three British officers had just been arrested in an hotel in Limoges. She had gone there and managed to get some information. Her story was, roughly, as follows. The operator, who had not yet recovered from his recent shock, had had the misfortune to make a slight error in behaviour when, by sheer bad luck, a couple of police-inspectors entered the hotel for a snap check. His anxiety did not pass unnoticed. He had been detained and, when Alexandre and the third man came to join him, they had walked into a trap. The discovery of the W/T transmitter in the luggage had put the lid on it and all three were in jail. Both Marie and I were stricken with grief at the thought that they should have been taken and especially after so short a time in the field.

I was, of course, by now getting hardened to news of people being arrested, just as a man in the trenches gets used to his pals being shot, but I was deeply affected by Alexandre's capture.

This brings up the question of what happened to our agents when they were taken. There was, of course, no comparison in this respect between the two zones.

In the occupied zone there was no reliable way of finding out what happened to an agent after capture. The Germans had every right to treat us as spies and put us to death. This is exactly what the English were doing to the few German agents who were infiltrated into the United Kingdom.

The Gestapo also had a reputation for inflicting various tortures on captives to force information out of them. This was made quite clear to agents who volunteered to go to the occupied zone. It was dramatized by the offering, on departure, of a lethal pill and the information for those who were religiously inclined that the Church had given a dispensation allowing a cornered agent to commit suicide without sin.

There was no publicity given to arrests and when a fellow-agent was taken, he most frequently just vanished. We had, at the time, every reason to think that after a number of torture sessions he was shot out of hand. The same applied to any of our local French recruits. It was our duty to make it quite clear to them that by associating with us they were running great risks and exposing themselves to torture and death.

For the record, it was not until after the war that we learned what happened. Some men had been shot soon after capture, some had been kept alive in jail or sent to concentration camps, others had been taken to Germany shortly before the liberation of France and put to death there. In a few cases this delayed death-sentence was not carried out. In another small handful of cases the Germans treated their captives as special prisoners of war. The poignant stories of those who escaped execution in the notorious concentration camps, Buchenwald, Mathausen and others, are now well known. My point is that during the occupation we did not really know what happened when a man was arrested by the occupation forces.

As soon as an agent was taken the most extraordinary rumours would immediately begin to circulate. The person who brought the news of the arrest would often give you all the details of how it occurred, whose fault it was, where the captive had been taken, where he was being detained, the size of his cell and what he got to eat for breakfast. A few days later someone else would give you an entirely different version on each point. It was vital to have a good estimate of the information the Gestapo would be able to derive from the capture. How much did he know? Even if he did not break down under interrogation, his examiners might be able to get a lead from the contents of his wallet, or a search of his home.

Every organizer remembers the catastrophes caused by diaries with names and addresses in clear, which, in spite of frequent warnings, some people would keep.

A good organizer would, therefore, whenever he learned of the arrest of a member of his circuit, order the breaking of normal connections with the arrested man's close contacts and advise the latter to change their place of residence immediately as a precaution.

He would then set up a watch to see if further raids followed the arrest. After a couple of weeks an estimate of the damage could generally be made.

I can assure you that this 'nosing around' to decide how far the 'contamination' had gone was a good exercise for the nerves! Each door seemed to bear a question-mark: Was it a mousetrap or not?

In the Z.N.O. (non-occupied zone) things were different. The Vichy police were very keen and active. However, when they did catch a 'resistant' they did not always know very well what to charge him with. The favourite headings seemed to be 'associating with criminals' and 'endangering the security of the State'. Vichy dared not start shooting British officers or their recruits, and apparently the old Marshal had put his foot down and would not hand them over to the Germans. Our agents were put in jail for the duration of the war and it was sometimes possible to find out where they were being held. In some cases escapes were organized. I have mentioned the early capture of a number of our agents, including George I, in a trap in Marseilles. After stages in various jails, they ended up in a camp at Meauzac. In the summer of 1942 an escape operation succeeded and they got back to England.

Among those who had been unfortunate enough to be taken in the unoccupied zone was a British agent who, like myself, had been dropped far from his target-point. He, however, landed on the roof of a gendarmerie! As he slid off the tiles his parachute was caught in the chimneys and he remained suspended in his harness high up against the wall. The gendarmes came out to investigate the noise and he was thus arrested before even reaching the ground. Under the circumstances there was little he could say to talk himself out of it.

When I heard of this hard-luck story, I became almost reconciled to my own forty-mile miss and twisted ankle.

Resistance in the Z.N.O. was intensifying and becoming better organized, but there were a great many instances of poor security. Too many of our people who should have been working independently of each other had fallen into the habit of meeting frequently.

It was, of course, very comforting to talk to one's friends, and co-operation made work easier, but it also meant that a single leak could flood the whole boat.

I found it hard to believe that the Germans had not organized an espionage network of their own in the Z.N.O. in preparation for a change of situation. It seemed to me that quite a number of resistance workers must already have been spotted.

In November 1942 my fears were to be proved well founded.

10. A munitions drop

THE life of a special agent was not quite all intrigue and disaster. Let us go to the country for a breath of fresh air.

We cannot forget the Gestapo, the Wehrmacht, the Vichy police or our luckless comrades; they are the background of our life, but we can relax while doing a healthy job.

Imagine you were a special agent and had ordered by W/T a delivery of stores at a place in the occupied zone about one hundred miles from Paris, for instance.

This means that at last you have access to a radio-operator who is functioning. You have reactivated your local contact in the area and together you have been to see one of the farmers you visited some months ago and told him to produce his team.

It is to be a small delivery—half a dozen containers only, but enough for your immediate targets in the area. It is to be their first experience in tangible resistance work, and this time you want on the ground only a handful of men so you can personally stress to each one the important points to be observed. You wish each man to be able later to conduct dropping operations himself, with larger teams he will have recruited.

The farmer has introduced you to his merry men: his son, a cousin of his, the latter's son-in-law, and an awful character—the local poacher—a real man of the woods who knows every tree and path and will prove invaluable as a scout.

Your local lieutenant and yourself will make up the half-dozen.

One man per container is not a bad ratio if you want to handle the stuff quickly. You have explained how the B.B.C. personal-message system works. You yourself will listen with your local lieutenant in town. The rest will listen at the farm.

As few operations are being carried out as yet, you are still able to ask the local people to compose their own message. What would they like? They are a bit shy about this—come on, anything will do—a funny one about the Boches, such as 'Hitler is losing his pants!' Defiance to Vichy—'Foch would never have surrendered!' A poetic phrase like 'How beautiful is our land!' Yes! your lieutenant says his wife would like that. Agreed then? Fine!

The farmer is already busy pouring out the wine for a toast to success as you choose a spot for the rendezvous. It is to be at the point where a pathway leads off a small road through a wood. There you and your lieutenant will meet the four other men, who know their way through the woods to the ground which a stranger could not possibly find at night.

The time is 2200 hours—curfew-time.

So you return to base to get your signal sent to London, stating your special requirements, the co-ordinates of the ground and the B.B.C. message.

Shortly afterwards you receive a reply confirming your instructions and advising that the operation will be 'On' during the next moon-period, say from the twentieth to the twenty-sixth and from 2300 hours to 0100 hours G.M.T. (In the summer months the limits were fairly close because of the few hours of darkness.)

You send a message with the dates to your lieutenant and join him at his house on the twentieth. He tells you all is ready. Yes! The farmer has the necessary torch-lamps for the signals. You will listen to the B.B.C. French news at 1930 hours while having dinner. If the message comes, the two of you will leave on bicycles at 2030 hours. As you are not a champion cyclist it is better to allow an hour and a half for the thirty kilometres to the rendezvous.

The farmer and his boys, who are only a few minutes from

there, will have listened to both the 1930 and the 2115 hours broadcasts before leaving and will be able to tell you whether the message was repeated in the second programme. If it was not, then you can all go and spend the night at the farm.

There is quite a bit of electricity in the air that evening as you sip your aperitif in the drawing-room with your lieutenant and his young wife. The news bulletin in French is just coming through the roar of the jamming, your friend turns the knobs seeking the best wavelength, and the clearest volume-tone combination. They don't take much interest in the latest bit of Anglo-American strategy! The news finally comes to an end. . . . 'And now here are a few personal messages. . . .' Your heads lean towards the set as if drawn by an ear. The first one is not yours— neither is the second, nor the third. Then: 'How beautiful is our land!—I repeat: How beautiful is our land!' There it is!

The young couple jump up excitedly. Their eyes are bright. For them it is the first manifestation of power. That text was composed here, unknown to anyone except a few initiates, and now it has just been shouted through millions of loudspeakers while still remaining *their* secret.

'Come on, you men had better get your dinner! You've no time to lose!' The pretty young wife has turned into the *vivandière* of the martial legends. A kind of ancestral instinct seems to dictate her hereditary rôle, which is to speed the males of the species on their warlike expeditions.

Later that warm evening you are on a bicycle picking your way through the suburbs of the town. Your companion wanted to take his car, but you have explained that if anything went wrong it would be too easily identified. You are now on the *route Nationale* for a mile or two and then on a *route départe-mentale*.

Although not a champion, you have done a great deal of cycling throughout your missions in France, enough to give you good wind and legs. You can enjoy fully the beautiful landscape as you rise heavily on the pedals to climb a hill and then go flying down the other side with the wind whistling past your ears.

As the sun sinks the fields and woods take on a russet colour and the eastern horizon merges into a misty blue. You engage in a bit of racing with your high-spirited companion, and then, as there is plenty of time to spare, you assume a more moderate cruising speed and recover your breath by filling your lungs with the pure air.

A few massive cows watch you gravely as you swish past. The scent of hay is strong. On this secondary road you meet very few people. A few farmhands returning from the fields on bicycles, a farmer with a horse and cart, and one motor-van. Your lieutenant can identify this as belonging to Monsieur so-and-so, who is in the timber business. You immediately take your friend up on this. . . . 'What did I tell you? . . . You can see for yourself how easily cars can be identified!' Yes, of course he does, but after all, we shall eventually need the motor-truck to transport the stuff away from the farm and certainly in the future if heavier deliveries are received. You explain that the motor-transport must be laid on only when we are sure the coast is clear. The important thing is that the motor-lorry must not be associated with the presence of the low-flying aircraft. The plane must arrive first. Bicycles will do for tonight. We'll see about the van tomorrow.

There are no Germans to be seen. You recall that some people, both at home and here, have found it hard to believe that parachutes can be dropped secretly from noisy aircraft without the garrisons being alerted for miles around. You indulge in a little arithmetic. What is the size of France: half a million square kilometres? In order to cover the ground effectively at night, the Germans would require 10,000 patrols. If a patrol were to find and attack a reception committee they would have to deal with resolute, armed men, who would be prepared to fight for their lives and who would know their way about the woods better than the soldiers.

The prospect of a bellyful of lead by moonlight was probably not a very attractive one. Therefore, even the toughest S.S. would not care to go into action in squads of less than a dozen, which would require guard posts of forty men.

From what distance can a blacked-out aircraft be seen at night under a full moon? Your previous experience leads you to say a thousand yards at most. How far can it be heard? Your opinion is not more than five miles. The clearing you are using tonight is well tucked away in the woods on high ground and all should go well.

As the sun sets the air grows cooler. Only the crackling of the small flints under your rubber tyres heralds your arrival at the rendezvous at the edge of the wood. You push your bicycles along the path under the trees. Some dark forms emerge from the shadow of the bushes and excited whispers tell you about hearing the B.B.C. message. Did it come through on the 9.15 programme also? Yes! it was on both broadcasts. 'How beautiful is our land.' They keep repeating it—this message they had picked themselves only a few days before! Just fancy! The mighty B.B.C. had obeyed their orders!

As you follow in single file between the tree-trunks one man tries to imitate the manner of the announcer another assures you that there was almost a sob in his voice—in any case, he read it better than any of the other personal messages—anyway, it was their first message.

When you arrive at the clearing it is 10.30; there is a wait of two and a half hours.

It is a bit of a bore, but it is better to sit around here than risk being seen on the roads after curfew.

You are thanking your lucky stars that the operation is 'On' the very first night, particularly since you're introducing new people to the work. Newcomers are discouraged if their job is postponed night after night and possibly until the next moon. You are only hoping that the plane will find you. You do not mention the possibility of errors in navigation. You use the time to instruct the team.

Three men are to stand in a triangle, with one summit pointing upwind. Each man will shine a white torch-light at the aircraft, and at the upwind apex there will also be a red light.

The aircraft is supposed to drop its load over the red-and-white point so that the wind will blow the 'chutes to land inside the triangle. There is almost no wind this evening, so the direction doesn't matter very much.

London never stated how big the triangle had to be, so you tell the men to stand fifty yards apart. (Later on the arrangement was changed to a straight row of three white lights with one hundred yards spacing.)

You give them what bit of technical data you have—the plane will be flying at 150 metres (500 feet) above the ground and rather slowly—just over 200 k.p.h. (about 130 m.p.h.).

You stress the fact that it is very important that each man should count the number of parachutes as they come down. The wind may rise and blow some of them into the trees. They can be difficult to find. Unless you know how many to look for, you might leave one or two lying about. On the other hand, you do not want to spend all next day combing the woods for an imaginary parachute.

As the low-voiced conversation progresses, the cousin's son-in-law reveals that he was in the French Air Force. He has done a lot of flying—and, frankly, he is sceptical about a navigator being able to find a particular field, such as this, at night, especially after a long voyage from England and, no doubt, a lot of attention from the German flak and perhaps fighters.

You retort: 'Wait and see—you don't know our boys!' You pray silently that there will be something to see and try to forget about previous errors of navigation. The aviator questions you further. 'Will the plane fly high over the coast?' 'No, on the contrary, they will come in low to increase the surprise effect.' Suddenly there is a concert of 'Sh, Sh, Sh. . . .' and you hear the drone of a plane. You look at your watch. It is only 11.30, an hour and a half to go yet. This is probably not yours.

The sound dies away.

The poacher has been patrolling in and out of the edge of the wood and reports all clear.

The moon has been up some time and the landscape is inundated by the silver light. You feel you could read a newspaper.

There is not a cloud in sight. The dark-blue dome of heaven, the brilliant constellations and the bright moon riding across them—what a setting for the most solemn mysteries! So men have thought since the beginning of time.

As your lieutenant is a scholar, you inform him that the organization's code name for the moon is not Phoebe, but Charlotte. Ah, yes! How many times you have been disappointed by radiograms which said, 'Regret operation impossible account state Charlotte. . . .'

The faint sounds of the insects and night-birds, some whispering from one of the team, the sigh of an occasional breath of night air in the trees, as if the world were breathing in its sleep . . . the luminous hands of your wrist-watch move slowly until at last it is one o'clock. This is zero hour.

You ask your companions to stop talking. A few minutes pass in silence. Then someone utters a 'Sh! Listen!' and raises a hand. You stiffen and stop breathing. False alarm. You take a few steps to relax. The luminous watch-hands seem to be moving quickly now. It is soon half past one, then a quarter to two.

Your companions are on the alert. You try to force your ears to listen even more intently. With all your senses you are sounding the blue-and-silver night.

'Sh! Quiet! Listen . . . listen! . . .'

You hear a faint sound, like a series of smothered grunts in the distance, 'grr . . . grr . . . grr . . . grr. . . .' They grow louder and join into a pulsating growl. 'Get to your posts! Switch on as soon as you see my own light!'

The men dash to the corners of the triangle. There is a muffled argument. 'Let me hold the lamp!' 'No! I will hold it first, then you can have it after!' 'Shut up, you kids!' (This is from the farmer—who is now once more the corporal of 1914.) The growl has swelled into a steady drone. You switch on your torch and point it towards the sound. The other lamps come on. The droning grows louder and develops a rhythmic beating.

You distinguish the high-pitched whine of reduction gears. You strain your eyes. It cannot be far off now.

There—that small black patch moving swiftly and steadily across the dark-blue sky! The roar increases in volume. The black object comes on towards you and becomes a great aeroplane which sweeps majestically very low over your heads, and slightly to one side of the lights, to the mighty descending organ-note of the exhausts.

Four engines—twin square rudders—it is a Halifax.

The machine vanishes into the night and the sound dies down to a soft droning.

The man standing nearest you asks excitedly: 'Is that it? Has it missed us?' 'Yes! It is ours right enough. The pilot has just made a dummy run over the target. Now he has to make a very wide turn and come back. Keep the lights pointing at the sound and, above all, count the parachutes. You had better run along and remind each man of this!'

Your messenger doubles off in the dimness and the droning begins to grow louder again. It is coming straight over you this time. The reflection of the moon makes a star of light on the perspex nose. The whirring of the propellers seems to make the heavens ring as you lean over backwards to look straight up.

Just as the machine is directly above it appears to explode into a spray of round black flowers, which remain tossing in its wake. You begin to count. One, two, three . . . five . . . eight parachutes, are floating down. As they near the ground you can distinguish the tubular containers which land with a tinny clonk. The dark canopies settle down delicately and flatten out gracefully on the earth, like balloons being deflated.

There is a general stampede towards the containers.

You find everyone pawing the metal cylinders and running their fingers through the silken parachute cords.

One of the team is sitting astride a container and patting it with both hands and saying, 'They are from our friends.'

You ask each man in turn how many 'chutes there were.

The majority say eight. 'Good, then let us find them. But listen, there is the sound of the plane again. It seems to be coming back. Perhaps there is something else. Quick! back to your posts and switch the lights on!' Sure enough, here it is again, a great black bird against the blue. However, it does not fly straight overhead, but sweeps close by in a broad turn. You understand that it is merely the crew of the aircraft who are wanting to have a look at you and see, if they can, whether they made an accurate drop. You have heard that the R.A.F. get a kick out of seeing their 'customers'. You collect your remnants of the Morse code and flash '*Merci*', 'O.K.', etc.

The bomber roars off into the night again and this time the sound dies away altogether. You return to the containers and explain to the flattered team that it was a complimentary extra lap, the R.A.F.'s way of saluting.

. It has been a good drop. The group of parachutes have fallen within a hundred yards of the lights. You count the containers and find only six. Where are the other two?

The form of a running man appears out of the dark. It is the poacher. He says there are two more parachutes on the edge of the clearing, hanging in the trees. That makes the eight. You go back with him and find, not two more containers, but two square canvas-covered packages. He climbs up the trees like a cat, opens his great clasp-knife and down come the 'chutes and parcels.

You rejoin the others and explain that the containers were slung in the bomb-racks of the plane—in fact, their length and diameter are the same as a 500-pound bomb—and were, therefore, dropped together in a bunch, whereas those two packages were thrown out through the hole by the dispatcher, which explains why they fell a short distance away.

The team watch intently as you show how the container is hinged all down one side and opens like a pea-shell when you unfasten the catches. Inside are three short, fat, cylindrical canisters which contain the equipment. They are heavy. On the lid of each are two wire handles for carrying. You gather the parachute canopy with its cords and push it into the now empty container-shell.

The old farmer says it is a pity we did not bring a wheel-barrow. Next time he will do so.

The heavy canisters are removed from all the containers and are being borne away through the trees to the opposite edge of the road. A shuttle service is organized. Some carry one canister at a time perched on one shoulder. Others try carrying them by the handles and discover what you know already: that those wire handles are the most horrible finger-cutters in the world! The old farmer, however, has come prepared. He removes his coat and unwinds a rope from around his middle, passes it through the handles and, using a stout stick, contrives a wonderful lifting tackle and swings off with his share of the load while the younger men watch with envy.

After a number of return trips all the canisters, the empty containers and the two separate packages are gathered together inside the thicket.

You open the two packages. They are heavily padded with sponge-rubber slabs. They generally contain special equipment.

One of ours contains a new radio-transmitter. In the other are a few special articles you have asked for. The container canisters will be filled with normal stores, explosives, arms, ammunition and some comforts.

Your equipment now has to be taken to the farm. As this is a first operation for this team, and you want them to be able to carry on for years, if necessary, you have decided to make a proper exercise of it and take full routine precautions.

The farmer and his son are to make their way back to the farm and wait for sunrise. They will then go out at their usual hour and get into conversation with the other early risers of the neighbouring village and find out whether any suspicions have been aroused. They will hang around for a couple of hours to make sure there are no unusual German patrols or snap raids in the neighbourhood, then harness the old horse to the cart and set out to bring in a few loads of fodder from the fields. This chore will naturally lead them to the place where you are waiting and the fodder will contain some unusual ingredients.

In the meantime you and the three others will be transferring the contents of the canisters to the sacks which have been provided

I

for that purpose. You will also be getting rid of the container-shells, empty canisters, parachutes, foam-rubber packing, etc., by burying them with the spades which the team have brought.

As you unpack the canisters your companions become quite excited. The machine-guns and automatic pistols, the ammunition and hand-grenades are familiar enough, but they wonder a little at the Sten, with its cheap, rough-and-ready finish. They are curious about the rolls of plastic explosive, the incendiary pots and the time-pencils, the detonators, the silvery coils of Cordtex, and all the other paraphernalia. They fire questions at you. 'And that, what is it? Is that really an explosive? It looks like plasticine,' etc. They are already planning raids. The poacher wants to go at once and set fire to the farm of a certain collaborator.

But you have something less grim to show them. In among the munitions are some of the all-important comforts: cigarettes, tobacco, slabs of chocolate, a jar of butter, a few tins of food. You hand out a small ration to each and a wonderful human relationship is established between the mysterious H.Q. in London and the local recruits. They are ready to believe that Winston Churchill himself had the cigarettes put in.

Dawn is in the sky. The bright sun rises.

Your lieutenant is nursing an assembled Sten-gun and drawing deeply on a cigarette. There is a faraway look in his eyes. This is a great moment in his life.

You issue each man a pistol and a box of ammunition. A patrol is sent to make sure no traces have been left on the dropping-ground. You superintend the burying of the container-shells and canisters and the supplies are now contained in a pile of sacks.

A delicate subject is broached: the parachute canopies are made of silk . . . it would be fine for underwear. You point out that they are dyed a greenish-brown for camouflage. You talk earnestly. The Boches have already captured some of the deliveries. They know what our equipment looks like. You do not know how good their security organization is, but in Britain descriptions would be circulated to all units. Now a parachute canopy is not just a single huge piece of silk. It is not even a number of plain panels each reaching from centre-hole to rim. Each panel is divided into a lot of small patches stitched together with stout hems so that a tear cannot split the whole panel.

These criss-crossing hems would show on a man's shirt, a lady's blouse, or an undershirt, no matter how cleverly made. Also, the braided, silken, parachute cords are very lovely, but also very special in appearance. . . .

They listen carefully and nod approval, but of one thing you can be sure . . . a couple of those damned canopies are already folded away somewhere, although you had them all paraded and counted before burial.

But how can you hope to keep tally of a few miserable parachutes when you're dealing with people who are capable of concealing such large substantial objects as cows and pigs from the authorities?

Perhaps, after all, you are being a bit fussy, so you let the matter drop with a weak warning that if any man gets caught because of a shirt made of parachute silk or a belt of parachute cord, you will not feel the least bit sorry for him.

One of the team, who has been keeping a watch, comes back to report that the horse and cart are already in view. You go to the edge of the wood. Sure enough, across the rolling fields you see the farmer and his son guiding their faithful animal slowly up the slope in your direction.

You can soon hear the creaking of the cart. They stop now and then to make their foraging look realistic and finally reach the edge of your thicket.

You say they have been very quick. They report that everything is in order. The villagers are asking each other whether they heard the *three* aeroplanes which flew over so very low last night. The strategists have proved, on a map, that the planes were headed for northern Italy, so everyone is satisfied. The farmer hands down a huge basket. It is your breakfast—a colossal meal. The farmer's wife had bawled them out for leaving the Englishman in the woods with nothing to eat and sent them back with masses of ham, hard-boiled eggs, bread, butter, cheese, several bottles of red wine, brandy, etc.

The two carters receive their rations of cigarettes and you all set to. Some of the sacks are loaded on the cart and covered over with fodder and off they go back to the farm. You dawdle over your breakfast until they return for a second trip. After the last trip you pick up your bicycles, return to the road and cycle to the farm.

You superintend the hiding away of the stuff and then enjoy a little rest and relaxation.

The whole team are elated and want some more. Now they have seen exactly what occurs, they begin to suggest improved arrangements. The discussion goes on right through a huge lunch.

If they receive larger deliveries they will need more men. Names of reliable people are suggested. You stress again and again the need for secrecy. It is better for the time being to receive small deliveries regularly and safely than a big one which would mean enlisting a lot of chatterboxes who would get everybody arrested. By taking care and trouble over the arrangements, para-chutings can take place without bother, as they have just seen. The great danger is, and always will be, careless talk and abnormal behaviour in public. The war may go on for years. There must be no rumours which may reach enemy ears within weeks or even months. The time for more open activities will surely come, but not just yet.

The ex-Air Force man is particularly enthusiastic. He is amazed that the plane found the field and keeps repeating: 'What navigation! Well, I'm convinced now.'

Yes! They are convinced. This first operation was their initiation. The B.B.C. French Programme had been urging resistance to the enemy, but how? Then one day you had made an appearance. You later returned and, lo and behold, here were the weapons and ammunition! Resistance had become a concrete reality.

It is a comforting moment for you too. You notice that your

friends are smiling warmly and respectfully at you, and realize that you have acquired a new status in their eyes. You have produced something tangible.

You listened to their profession of faith in victory.

You beckoned and some of the glorious airmen of the legendary Royal Air Force mounted their great machine and came flying through the night, rushing the enemy defences with a 5000 h.p. roar of defiance.

They risked their lives, not to bomb some major target selected by a council of generals, but to find that little clearing chosen by humble country-folk.

So from now onwards your mark is made, your prestige established. Your laziness will pass for that wonderful English phlegm, your failures for long-term strategy, and any acts of stupidity which would immediately brand anyone else as a superlative clot are ascribed to superior, if incomprehensible, cunning. (I used to take immediate advantage of my new prestige by allowing the others to carry all the heaviest packages.)

Your lieutenant says he will arrange for his motor-lorry to pick up the supplies in two days' time and take them to your arms depot in town. Now he has seen the bulk of the stuff, he can finish the false floor he has been designing, between the chassis frames. It will form an invisible storage space.

You settle the details of the next operation and finally in the late afternoon, after much hand-shaking and congratulation, heavy with good food and wine, you mount your bicycle and set out knowing you can count on this team until the end of the war.

Your lieutenant has a small parcel of some of the airborne comforts—chocolate, butter, etc., for his wife. He says that they will be proof that it was with an English plane that he spent the night!

As you pedal away in the bright warm sunlight, you look at the beautiful landscape, the deep furrows, the abundant woods, the strong cattle and feel that the enemy may well covet them, but will not be able to take them all away. In fact, once those lads back there get into their stride, he will get a jolly sight less of the good things than he is expecting—and quite a few bad things instead. . . .

And so you go back to the city—to intrigue, suspicion and news of the latest arrests.

11. Lysander

UNTIL I returned to London a second time, in October 1942, I was very busy with the usual special agent's work. I met a number of very interesting people, moved about a good deal, and had a few narrow escapes.

I was to return by air this time in what was known as a 'pick-up' or the 'Lysander' operation, named after the type of aircraft generally used for this purpose.

Many people found it extraordinary that an Allied plane could actually land in enemy territory and take off again with passengers, but such landings were no novelty. I believe they were already made during the 1914-18 war.

In those days, of course, the biplane aircraft used could land in a large field and detection devices were rather crude.

A modern fast monoplane needs a long clear strip and adequate signalling on the ground. I know of at least one Lysander operation taking place as early as 1941.

These landings were arranged when it was wished to bring agents home quickly to report and advantage was generally taken of these trips to send out agents who were ready to go, especially those who, for one reason or another, were unable to parachute.

The R.A.F. ran a special training course for landing operations and only those agents who had passed it were authorized to organize a 'pick-up'.

The field had first of all to be satisfactory from the security point of view—away from roads, railways, inhabited buildings, etc. It had then to provide three clear avenues, each 600 yards long and at an angle of sixty degrees to each other, so the aircraft could land whatever the direction of the wind.

These avenues or landing-strips had to have firm, even surfaces and the grass must not be too long and there must be no holes or furrows. Moreover, beyond the ends of each strip, any obstacles such as fences, hedges, trees, etc., had to be so low or far away that the aircraft could fly in on a slope as shallow as one in fifty, if necessary.

Finding such a field in France was quite a job.

On several occasions I made journeys out to the country to inspect grounds which had been reported by people 'who had been aviators' and claimed to know all about flying, only to be shown small patches which only a helicopter could have used. Other 'aviators' asked whether it *really* mattered if the earth was ploughed up for sowing potatoes!

Sometimes I did see an apparently ideal expanse and paced it out only to finally discover that it just failed to meet all the requirements.

There were a number of disused flying-fields, but these were generally either guarded, obstructed, or ploughed up.

In fact the enemy would usually have any promising-looking tract of land ploughed up or otherwise obstructed.

The best areas for seeking grounds were pasture-lands in the bends of rivers, such as the Loire or the Saône. Some immense meadows were to be found there.

When an apparently flawless ground had been found, its location and description had to be radioed to London. The R.A.F. would later send an observation plane to take a photograph. If the experts approved it, it would be given a code name and there was another way home.

As with a dropping operation, a 'pick-up' would be 'laid-on' for a certain moon-period and the usual B.B.C. message system would be used. When the right words came through the reception committee and the outgoing passenger or passengers (two was the normal number) would proceed to the ground that night. Let us follow them. The bicycles are hidden in a thick wood. The organizer determines the direction of the wind and selects the corresponding landing-strip. The skeleton 'flare-path' is then paced out—it is a very simple affair. Two hundred yards from the downwind end of the landing-strip a first stick is driven into the ground. A second one is stuck one hundred and fifty yards upwind of the first. A third stick is planted fifty yards square to the right of the second one facing upwind. An extinguished electric torch is fixed to the top of each stick.

The plan is that the Lysander will touch down opposite the first lamp and to the right of it and finish its landing run between the two other lamps.

The organizer takes his stand near the first stick and carries a fourth lamp in his hand for signalling. The two passengers stand near him. Their luggage consists of a couple of brief-cases stuffed with documents. They have given away all their clothing to fellow-agents and recruits. One assistant is ready to go to the other end of the flare-path, near the second lamp. An ingenious feature is that the first torch, known as 'A', has its reflector removed and is tied to the top of the stick so that the naked bulb can shine in all directions. The other two torches, 'B' and 'C', have been tied to the sticks in such a way that they shine their beam towards 'A' only.

Thus the pilot will see all three lights clearly and simultaneously only when he approaches from the correct direction for landing.

The party of four are waiting in the dark as the moon rises. Now and then they go through an extraordinary performance. Since pasture-lands are particularly suitable for landing operations dark forms sometimes loom out of the night and the men find themselves surrounded by cows staring patiently at these nocturnal trespassers.

The dull clonk of a cowbell can be heard as one of the animals moves closer to get a better look. One of the party whispers that if these cows are standing on the landing-strip when the plane comes, the result may be disastrous. The party start hopping towards the great animals with waving arms and much fearful hissing and shooing. The cows gallop off clumsily into the dark with their bells clonking. The midnight cowboys find their way back to lamp 'A' to resume their vigil. Two minutes later they can distinguish the black shapes of the cows once more standing in a circle around them.

Zero hour has arrived. Lysanders are usually on time so there will probably be only a few minutes to go.

Sure enough, there is the drone of a plane. The organizer points his torch in the direction of the sound and flashes his personal recognition signal: dash, dot, dash, dash—'Y' for Yvonne. Out of the blue appears a small black aeroplane with a more complicated shape than a bomber.

The signal lamp under the fuselage flashes the agreed answering signal: dot, dash, dot, dot—'L' for London. That's it, no mistake. As the plane passes over the field, its long, narrow dragonfly wings can be clearly recognized.

The organizer switches on lamp 'A' and, seeing this, his assistant lights 'B' and sprints across to light 'C'.

The 'Lizzie' circles the field, clearly silhouetted against the few silvery clouds. It has been possible to distinguish the torpedo-like extra petrol-tank slung under the fuselage and the large wheel-fairings which make a 'Lizzie' look as if it were wearing a pair of Russian boots. It disappears and can be heard purring away in the distance for a minute. Then suddenly it becomes visible again, coming in very low towards the field. Its landing lights come on and cast a great pool of light on the grass. It howls past light 'A', turning the silent secretive darkness into a roaring aerodrome. The engine note drops to a stuttering and the plane with lowered tail sinks to the ground away towards light 'B'.

The bump as its strong wheels hit the grass can just be heard, the landing lights are switched off, and it becomes almost invisible against the background of the distant trees. A roar from the engine and 'Lizzie' has turned and reappears taxi-ing towards the waiting travellers. It rolls right up to 'A', swings round and stops facing upwind, with a comfortable bubbling sound from its exhaust. The helmeted pilot can be clearly seen in the cockpit.

The organizer and the two homebound travellers move towards the fuselage aft of the high wing in the slip-stream of the idling propeller. The transparent after canopy has been slid backwards and the two incoming passengers are climbing over the side.

The second one hands down two suitcases to his fellow-traveller, who has already got out, and then jumps to the ground himself.

The first of the homebound passengers climbs up. (This machine has no ladder, only footholes in the side of the fuselage.)

The second man passes up their two brief-cases. Arms and legs disappear into the cockpit—the sliding hood moves forward and slams shut.

. The organizer and the two arrivals step back as the engine opens up and the plane moves forward. After a very short run the Lysander is off the ground and climbing steeply. A few moments later it is out of sight and the drone of its engine dies away.

Darkness, quiet and secrecy return to the field as the organizer and his assistant switch off the lights, uproot the sticks and lead the two arrivals across the fields to the bushes where the bicycles are hidden. The operation has lasted only six minutes!

As they go the newcomers are whispering personal greetings from people at H.Q. and the latest news from home.

·   ·   ·   ·   ·

When my companion and I had climbed into the after cockpit one night in October 1942, I found the handle and pulled the sliding hood forward over our heads and yelled 'O.K.' at the top of my voice. The engine opened up and we began to move. The amazing flying qualities of the machine were immediately obvious.

The men on the ground and the lights seemed to slide and drop away after the shortest of runs, almost as if, like a bird, we had flown straight off from the spot where we had been standing.[1]

[1] In point of fact, the take-off run was only about 150 yards and took only a few seconds.

We were sitting side by side on a wooden seat, facing the tail. The normal petrol-tank separated us from the pilot, who was in front. We had the most splendid visibility I have ever enjoyed from any aeroplane. We were enclosed under the transparent perspex canopy which sloped down towards the low tail, so that our view was uninterrupted sideways, overhead, astern, and largely below. There were parachutes in the cockpit and we fumbled to adjust them. I found difficulty in getting my harness tight enough and hoped I should not have to use it.

After admiring the nocturnal scenery for some time I tried to recall the correct drill for Lysander passengers.

The main thing was to keep a look-out astern for German night-fighters. We had no guns, but ample defensive armour in the form of extreme manœuvrability.

Provided he received warning, the pilot could dive, turn and twist the Lysander out of the way of any Messerschmitt. I gathered that the only risk for the passengers would be that of dying of fright during such aerobatics.

I found the intercom headphones with their microphone and switch, put them on, moved the switch and said hello to the pilot. He said hello, but if I was all right I had better keep it switched off as it sputtered in his ears. I tried to determine which course we were following by studying the rivers and lakes which are so clearly visible from the air at night. I also kept watching the sky and suddenly saw a small black shape which looked like a bird flying alongside us opposite the wing-tip. This must be a fighter taking a look at us first. I carried the microphone to my face and was just trying to figure out which side was 'port' or 'starboard' when one was facing backwards when a white cloud threw the 'enemy' into relief, and I realized it was the streamlined insulator of the wireless aerial which, in this aircraft, was stretched between the port wing-tip and the tail! My finger jumped away from the intercom switch as if it had been red-hot! As I was apparently no good at spotting Messerschmitts I returned to admiring the unique moonlight scene. After an hour and a half the coast appeared. Away to the east was the black mass of a great headland I could easily identify as the northern bank of the Seine estuary with Le Havre and Sainte-Adresse.

We must have crossed the coast somewhere near Cabourg. There was no flak at all. The land quickly faded and we were over the Channel.

By pressing my face to the side I could get quite a good three-quarter forward view and soon another dark coast-line appeared ahead of us. Some lights came on suddenly on the ground a little way inland—white and red—in a pattern which obviously meant something to the pilot for we began to lose height and turn.

A few minutes later we came to a stop in a dispersal area where some uniformed figures and a car were waiting in the dark. Two officers from our H.Q. stepped forward to greet us. My travelling companion and I turned to thank our pilot, who had just alighted from his cockpit, and then got into the car which ook us to enjoy a whisky-and-soda in the mess of Tangmere aerodrome.

12. Third mission

BEING suddenly transplanted from France to England produced a feeling of strangeness greater than going the other way.

The reasons for this could form the subject of an interesting psychological study. It was like arriving in another world. The uniform I now donned was my holiday suit! For everybody except the members of the organization I had to have a 'cover-story' just like a spy! Mine was that I had been on a technical mission to the Middle East. There was a kind of nervous reaction too, probably due to the sudden release of the pressure of being ever on the alert and living under a false name.

It is very difficult to recapture the atmosphere now, but in those years Paris, to Londoners, seemed as remote as the moon. Yet one day I could be walking along the Grands Boulevards among the Germans and the next morning strolling down Regent Street, having in the meantime taken an afternoon train to a place near Angers and flown over the same night.

An interesting study could also be made of the impressions of Frenchmen arriving in London.

It was possible by now for an agent to arrange for a promising recruit, who had proved himself by doing good work, to be sent to England for training as a special agent. If he qualified he was granted a commission in the British Army. He would then be parachuted back into France to start a circuit of his own. I was privileged to have several of my own local recruits flown to England. Their first day in London was like a dream. They were impressed at being able to obtain cheap meals in any restaurant without food coupons, and seeing the pats of butter on the table, small as they were. They would also enjoy the forgotten experience of buying packets of cigarettes and leaving quite long butts in the ashtrays, which nobody would empty into a little box. London at that time was the heart of the world. The efforts of all the democratic nations were being controlled from Whitehall. Even the Americans were building up huge military establishments in Britain, as their own mighty contribution to victory must of necessity take the form of operations launched from our shores. His Majesty's Prime Minister, Winston Churchill, was directing the gigantic preparations.

Officers and men from the Armed Forces of many nations were being trained in the use of the most modern weapons and scientific devices in the atmosphere of old-world traditional England. The British regiments had, in peace-time, caused on the Continent a certain amount of friendly amusement with their spit-and-polish, ceremonial red tunics, bearskins, colourful kilts and multiple brass badges. But the British Army had also produced the only practical modern uniform, the battle-dress, which all other armies were either adopting as it was, or at least slavishly copying.

Our French friends were therefore spirited into our midst and found themselves in a British uniform and with a bogus English name. This was necessary in order to protect their families in France. Had there been a leakage it might have proved fatal for them if the enemy had learned that the husband or father had gone to England.

It was fully realized that the Germans could be beaten only by a coalition of the great powers of the world which must outnumber them by three to one, at least, and it was obvious the Russians and the Americans were providing the superiority in numbers. However, only the poor old British and French nations had taken the initiative of declaring war on the Nazi bullies. The huge, mighty American and Soviet republics had waited until they were *attacked* and, like ourselves, taken a thrashing at the start.

Britain had fought *alone*—the others had not. It was, therefore, natural that our newly arrived French guests should feel proud to wear our uniform and exhilarated by their training courses in our special schools.

The transition from an existence under the invader's heel to the intense preparation for action filled them with eagerness. The parachute course was the thrilling climax of their hard training— the parachute was the symbol of subversive warfare, the link between the island stronghold and their own occupied soil.

The war situation was to change dramatically in this autumn of 1942. Alamein, the landings in French North Africa, and Stalingrad had swelled the list of famous historical events.

The great orator once more found the right words: 'Not the beginning of the end—but the end of the beginning.'

Special agents in France were no longer the representatives of a nation which was stubbornly warding off defeat, but the heralds of future victory.

When the Allies landed in Algiers the most immediate change as far as our organization was concerned was the invasion by the Germans of the former unoccupied zone. As this occurred in November 1942, I was still in England, having returned the previous month. Bad news began to arrive. A large part of our organization was smashed.

As I feared, the Germans had had their eyes on a number of our people and one of their first actions was to pounce on them. Some were known to have been arrested by the Gestapo, some disappeared and managed to get to Spain. Some of these were in Spanish jails, but might well be released. Among them were some agents who had been arrested earlier by the Vichy authorities and turned loose when the Germans crossed the demarcation line. These releases were the subversive counterpart of the scuttling of the French warships at Toulon.

Meanwhile I was preparing for my return to France in early 1943.

The organization had grown. We had all kinds of new gadgets. We were even issued with imitations of French

'Gauloises' cigarettes in their blue packages. They had only one defect; they were slightly too long. There were also imitation French matchboxes.

The most important development, however, was that H.Q. had managed to train a sufficient number of radio-operators for each organizer to have his own link. The circuits could thus operate independently.

I would be taking my own operator with me. He was a charming young R.A.F. flying-officer named Denis John Barrett, and quite bi-lingual. His field name was Honoré.

When we were introduced I explained my plans for keeping completely clear of other circuits. However, during the final briefing I was asked to make one contact with another organizer as soon as I arrived. Both the briefing officer and myself laughed as we discussed this inevitable 'exception which proved the rule'.

This time it was necessary that a new set of crystals be sent to the wireless-operator of a very important organizer called Prosper, and they wanted them delivered by hand of officer. These crystals were small carefully calibrated pieces of quartz which by their frequency rigidly determined the wavelength. They were moulded inside a sheath with pronged terminals and looked just like those porcelain cartridge-fuses familiar to householders. The operator when transmitting plugged the correct one for the scheduled frequency into his set.

It was therefore arranged that Honoré and I would be dropped near Blois to a small reception committee commanded by one of Prosper's lieutenants who would tell me how to contact his chief in Paris. When this had been done we would be free to proceed on our own mission.

One fine April evening the two of us left in a Halifax all to ourselves. We were taking two W/T transmitters as a precaution. In addition to our luggage packages, there were also a few containers in the bomb-bay for the reception committee.

This time the journey was uneventful and we were well looked after all the way by the dispatcher. When there were only

K

a few minutes to go the captain sent us his personal wishes for success and good luck, the exit-hole cover was raised, the news came that the ground lights had been sighted and once again I was squatting on the edge, looking across the hole at Honoré whose face was faintly illuminated by the dim light reflected upwards from the landscape which was rushing past 500 feet below. Red light—Honoré's legs hanging down the side—green light—down he had gone—down I went—the blast of wind—this time I found myself for a second lying flat on my back looking at the underside of the tail—then the Halifax seemed to be snatched away, I turned a somersault and found myself looking upwards again, but this time at my open parachute canopy and my own feet which were caught in the rigging!

I cursed myself for being a clumsy ass and managed to extricate my extremities. This allowed me to assume a correct attitude before hitting the ground. It was not quite the landing the instructor had taught me, but I was unhurt.

There was something unforgettable about the first few minutes after a secret parachute jump. The relief from the inevitable apprehension and the noise and confinement in the aircraft—the sweet cool air—the eerie beauty of the moonlit landscape—the majesty of the starry sky—the scent of the earth—the quietness—the thrill of adventure—all these elements were there. . . .

When I had removed my harness I rolled up my 'chute and carried it back along the line of flight. I soon saw two dark figures coming to meet me. I caused them some alarm by dropping to the ground to see them against the skyline, quite a routine precaution. They hoarsely whispered, 'No, no, don't shoot, we are friends.' I got up and a second later we were warmly shaking hands.

They led me to Honoré and the third 'receptionist', Prosper's lieutenant, Pierre Culioli. Honoré was unhurt, the containers were well grouped on the ground, but the two packages had landed some distance away in the trees. We wanted those packages badly as they contained our personal luggage and Honoré's precious

W/T sets. As there were only three of them, the leader asked whether Honoré and I were too tired to give a hand with the containers. All five of us set to work. The empty shells and cells were carried some distance away and thrown down a disused well. They made quite a din as they banged against the sides and finally crashed at the bottom, but our hosts said it did not matter. We moved the sacks of supplies to a safe hiding-place.

Our hard night's work was enlivened by a political argument between the two farmers. They were friends but one was a democrat and the other a Communist. It was funny to watch them lifting a container together and hoarsely gasping doctrinaire broadsides at each other.

Théo, the 'democratic' farmer, and I happened to be carrying a heavy canister between us. He asked me if I would not mind changing sides as one of his hands was not so good. I thus found out that he had been wounded in the 1914–1918 war. There was a lump in my throat as I reflected that this man was again serving his country by partaking in this new, weird warfare.

At dawn we went to the Communist's farm. His wife was waiting and gave us a huge breakfast. When the sun was fully risen we went to beat the woods along the line of flight and finally located the missing packages and parachutes hanging in the trees.

Théo then went off and eventually produced a small motor-van driven by a friend of his[1] in which Honoré and I, with our luggage, were taken to his own farm at Les Maisons Rouges, near Contres, which is south of Blois, in that lovely wine-producing and tobacco-growing region.

There was another huge meal and much wine and in the afternoon we laid down to rest. That evening Pierre Culioli brought us the latest information. We were told that the man-hunt for forced labour for Germany had been intensified and people were required to carry still one more document: a certificate from an employer. Anyone found to be unemployed was fair

---

[1] Henri Chartier, the driver, is now the greatly respected Mayor of Contres; the dynamic Théo Bertin is a forceful town councillor.

game for the press-gang! I made a note to procure some such
papers for Honoré and myself as soon as possible.

We now had to get to Paris and contact Prosper. I decided
to leave the two W/T sets with Théo for a few days; I wanted to
take advantage of this trip to make arrangements for transporting
them as safely as possible.

The next morning Honoré and I with our personal luggage
took a motor-bus from the nearest village to Blois, where we
boarded an express for Paris. I went to the address in the avenue de
Suffren which Culioli had given me.

The flat was occupied by a charming old lady and her
daughters. They made me welcome and summoned a young lady
called Denise who was one of Prosper's couriers. She said her
chief was away, but due back that same day in the late afternoon,
and she would take me to meet him at the Gare Saint-Lazare. We
were there when he arrived. I explained my errand and handed
him the crystals.

—Thanks. Is there anything I can do for you?

—I don't think so. I have my own W/T operator and I'll soon
be on my way to Troyes.

—I'm glad to meet someone who believes in the self-contained
unit! Nevertheless I'd like to put you in touch with someone
who has a friend in Troyes. He might be useful. I'll see you
avenue de Suffren tomorrow.

Prosper was in charge of a very big circuit which had ramifica-
tions all over the northern zone. I was impressed by his dynamic
personality.

On leaving the station I called on my regular Parisian contacts
who began to arrange for other contacts in the Troyes area. I also
learned that there seemed to be a flap on in Paris. There always
had been snap checks all over the city, but they seemed unusually
frequent just now. You went round a corner and there would be a
line of French policemen drawn across the street. Behind them
would be a number of German plain-clothes men. These were
the ones to beware of. If you were carrying some compromising
object in a parcel and hesitated at the sight of the cordon or

changed direction they would pounce on you. It was much better to walk straight on towards them and risk it.

Another favourite place for snap checks was inside main Metro stations. As Parisians will remember, it was difficult to avoid the police waiting in the underground passages to demand papers, frisk people and open parcels. Going down the steps from the sunlit boulevard and being unexpectedly challenged in a narrow corridor felt like entering a rat-trap.

There was even a retaliatory movement afoot among the Parisian population to encourage everybody to make a point of carrying parcels containing some perfectly useless, innocent stuff, in order to clutter up the barrages and give the police a lot of work for nothing.

All this convinced me that just now it would be worth while taking a bit of trouble in order to get Honoré's transmitters to Troyes without carrying them through Paris.

We were made comfortable that night by the charming old lady and next day Prosper came to see us.

There were several other visitors. When Prosper had dealt capably with their various problems, I remarked that there seemed to be too many of us in one flat.

He heartily agreed, but what could he do? London kept sending people to him, some of whom told their own friends how to reach him and there was a 'Special Agents Club' again. The same old story. The small world of resistance rallied to a strong personality, to one who would never refuse help and assistance.

We went out for a quiet beer in a café and then met the man he had mentioned in our first interview.

This meeting showed that the world of resistance was indeed small, for the man was none other than 'Cinema' who had been recruited long ago by Gauthier, the elder brother of poor Lucas. He was one of the men I had intended to see on my own anyway!

He had been nicknamed 'Cinema' because his real name was Gary and through the association of ideas: Gary—Gary Cooper—Cinema!

Prosper and I made an arrangement for contacting each other in the event of a grave emergency only and then parted. This was unfortunately the last time I ever saw that fine man Major Suttill, alias Prosper.

When I next met 'Cinema' he was with a tall, lean, broad-shouldered, handsome, aristocratic young man named Pierre Mulsant. I explained what was expected of him: the first thing was to get Honoré and his W/T sets installed in Troyes.

.   .   .   .   .

Shortly before noon Honoré and I were having coffee in a drivers' café outside Brie-Comte-Robert on the road to Troyes. At the stroke of twelve a charcoal-burning lorry drew up.

The powerfully built driver got out and came into the café proclaiming a thirst. I commented on the sultriness of the weather and we began to chat. I asked whether he could not give my friend a lift to the next town. He agreed—this sort of hitch-hiking was quite usual.

So, after I had paid for his drink, Honoré with his luggage and the precious suitcase with the broken handle were loaded into the lorry. I whispered to the driver that it was the latter package which was the valuable one.

He grinned reassuringly and said that he would hide it properly and see that Honoré and luggage were safely delivered to his boss.

When the lorry had gone wheezing and snorting on its way I sauntered back into the town and waited for the Paris-bound bus, thinking as I went what a nuisance that broken-handled suitcase had been. . . .

I was so sick of things going wrong that I decided to take ten times the necessary precautions, even if I did look silly. Pierre Mulsant was managing his father-in-law's business and could arrange for a motor-lorry, driven by a trustworthy driver, to make a return trip to Paris. Its movements, however, were confined to the direct road. Then I would make it my own business to see that the sets were brought there for a rendezvous at that café.

I had taken leave of the ladies, thanking them for their warm hospitality. They said that on some days they received so many visitors that the other tenants of the building must be beginning to wonder. Fortunately the concierge was a friend.

Honoré was now staying with pre-war friends at Bois-Colombes, so I returned to the farm at Maisons Rouges to see Théo and collect our hidden equipment. Into a large suitcase I packed the two transmitters and some other items. I also took a pistol and some ammunition. While in France I never carried a gun unless I had some other compromising object with me. If I were stopped and searched while carrying a bagful of weapons or a transmitter, the fat would be in the fire anyway, so I might as well have a chance of shooting it out.

These secret wireless-transmitters were marvellous instruments. Each one consisted of a small box about eight inches square and about three inches deep (I have forgotten the exact dimensions) which fitted into the smallest of fibre attaché-cases while leaving a space for stowing the headphones, aerial and a few other accessories. The upper panel carried the dials, tuning knobs, plugs, terminals, etc.

It was, however, quite heavy and my suitcase containing the two attaché-cases with the sets and other articles was a real burden.

I took the local bus back to Blois, boarded the Paris express, but at Orleans changed to a stopping train and alighted at Ablon, about ten miles south of Paris. I had chosen this roundabout way to avoid Paris and so far had had no trouble. There were no transverse trains or buses, so I set out on foot to carry my bag the nine miles to a small town called Boissy Saint-Léger, where I could get a bus for Brie-Comte-Robert.

It was one of the hardest marches that I have ever accomplished. A heavy suitcase is always awkward to carry, but after a mile or so the handle broke loose under the weight and added to my misery.

I cursed the London office for giving us cheap luggage, which was quite unfair as no luggage was made to stand such a strain.

The reader may well ask why I had not arranged for transport for this part of the trip. The answer is that I had tried to do so while in Paris, but in the short time available I had been unable to find someone who both had a vehicle and was willing to carry a 'death-penalty'. These things took time to arrange, and I was in a hurry to get it over.

Eventually I did reach Boissy Saint-Léger in the late afternoon and found a bus which put me down in a blinding rainstorm at Brie-Comte-Robert. I went to a local hotel for the night. The rendezvous at the café was at noon the next day. As I left the hotel to go there I was followed by a nasty-looking character I had noticed in the bar.

He accosted me and said my bag seemed to be heavy—was I going far?

I snapped that I was taking the bus to where I had to go and that I did not need a porter. He sheered off but I watched carefully to make sure he was not following. I had reached the café at the end of the town on the road to Troyes, a few minutes before Honoré appeared, having come straight from Paris.

During the ride back I relaxed in the luxury of having no more compromising luggage and, while viewing the assortment of suitcases, crates and boxes which my fellow-passengers were taking, began to rate myself for probably having gone to a lot of unnecessary trouble and got tired out for nothing.

However, as we were entering Paris, the bus was stopped by police and thoroughly searched and all articles of luggage opened. Well, maybe this would not have happened the previous day, but it did make me feel better.

Two days later I was in Troyes. Pierre and Honoré were waiting for me. The first job was to find premises for living and working. In a very short time we had a small flat on the outskirts for Honoré, an empty house in another suburb for my arms depot, a room in town where I lived and several houses to which we could go and in which Honoré could operate his wireless-set.

My engineer friends in Paris sent us two shining, brand-new bicycles.

Of course, Pierre Mulsant's house was open to us at all times. His wife Raymonde was a particularly beautiful blonde young woman. She was charming and seemed amused rather than alarmed by her two unusual guests. She played the piano very well and Honoré also had some skill on the keyboard, so we had quite a bit of music.

The 'cloak and dagger' slang word for a radio-operator had now become 'pianist'. I therefore had a 'pianist' who was also a real one.

13. Pianists and mutes

HONORÉ could transmit either from his own lodgings or one of our other safe houses. The precautions and procedure to be used were always the same.

Each operator had a 'plan', i.e. a kind of complicated time-table from which he could work out the dates and times when the home station would call and listen for him, and on which wavelengths. (He could transmit on any one of several by using the appropriate crystal.) The plan also determined the call signs and several other items.

These transmission times were called schedules or 'skeds'.

I seem to remember that the normal number was four or five a week. It was, of course, possible to ask for special extra schedules and these were generally granted.

If, for instance, I had nothing much to say at the time of a normal 'sked', but expected to have something important a few hours later, I would ask the operator to demand an 'extra-sked' for such a time; also if I needed a rapid reply to a question and did not wish to wait forty-eight hours. Each operator had his own code (purists claim that the correct term is 'cipher', but we always referred to 'the code') and this also was complicated. For the greater part of the war it was of the 'poem' type and carried in the operator's head.

It was recommended that messages should not exceed thirty or forty words (a word being a group of five letters) in order to keep the transmission time as short as possible, but it would frequently take the operator nearly an hour to encode such a signal—and longer to decode an incoming one.

Therefore, a 'pianist' obviously had a great deal of 'office-work' to do but this was not all. Our 'pianists' appeared to be able to work the Morse key and take down incoming messages at the rate of about fifteen or seventeen words a minute. Simple arithmetic would thus seem to show that the outgoing message would be sent in a couple of minutes and an incoming one taken down in about the same time, making a 'sked' last about five minutes in all, but this was rarely what actually occurred.

As the hour approached the set was opened on a table, the aerial (usually an inside one) fixed across the ceiling of the room, the earth connection secured to a water-pipe, and the power lead plugged into a light socket. The paper with the outgoing message, a ruled pad for taking the incoming one, and several sharpened pencils were lying beside the set.

At zero hour the operator would begin to tap out his personal call sign of the day on the key. He would then listen with his headphones and twiddle some knobs, then continue with the call sign and listen again. This would go on for a short while when suddenly a shrill piping would come from the earphones and he would say, 'There they are—calling—but they have not heard me yet.'

He would keep tapping on the key and listening, then suddenly jump in his chair. 'They have heard me!' More twiddling of knobs, some exchanges of information in the three-letter groups of the International Code: 'I am hearing you on strength four,' 'I have a message for you,' etc.

After a few moments of this the index finger of his free hand would point to the beginning of the encoded message, then move quickly along the meaningless jumble of letters pausing at each one while his other hand was furiously working the Morse key. The message was going out. Then the piping in the headphones would apparently ask for a repetition of some parts, for the finger would go back and return over the same groups again. Eventually he would push the text aside, pick up a pencil and poise it over the ruled writing-pad. 'They have a message for us too.' To the twittering of the headphones he would begin to print letters in the ruled squares of the pad, every now and then breaking in to ask for a repeat of some parts. Bit by bit neat groups of five letters each would appear on the paper until there were several lines of them. At last he would drop the pencil, there would be a further exchange of conventional signals between the key and the headphones and the tired operator would switch off the set, tear off the headphones and sit back with a sigh of relief.

The 'sked' had lasted half an hour.

The aerial would be taken down, and the set hidden with all its accessories.

Then the decoding would begin. As I have said, an hour might elapse before this was finished. It was rare that a decoded incoming message was not more or less garbled.

Occasionally only a few letters were wrong, but in many cases a considerable amount of guesswork and puzzling was necessary before the organizer could decide what was probably meant. Sometimes the poor 'pianist' would have to decode it all over again and again. I suppose they had much the same trouble at the home station with their reception.

It must be remembered that our sets were very low-powered, and that we had generally to use indoor aerials. Also, for various largely undiscovered reasons, the quality of reception and transmitting varied considerably from one part of the country to another and from one day to the next.

On some 'skeds' it was impossible to make contact at all and the poor sweating operator would rattle away at the key and twist the knobs in vain and have to give it up.

And what was the enemy doing about all this? We knew they had a network of listening stations for picking up illicit transmissions.

When one of these was heard, the direction-finding equipment could determine the area where it was situated. Local mobile D/F vans would then patrol the neighbourhood and try to pin-point the building in which it was operating.

One of the jobs of resistance workers was to identify these D/F vans which might be camouflaged as commercial vehicles.

I do not know how efficient this direction-finding was or how many of our operators were taken as a direct result of it. My own opinion at the time was that they could only define an area several hundred yards square. In a city this meant any one of several hundred buildings containing thousands of dwellings. I believed that from there onwards they had to resort to the jolly good old methods: spotting suspicious-looking individuals, using treachery, careless talk, and making sudden raids.

In a village or any area where buildings were few in number it was foolish to transmit for too long from the same place.

One operator told me there was a 'ground-wave' [sic] which extended for several miles around the set, making it detectable from near and showing the D/F vans that they were 'warm' but that if one moved away out of the range of this the set could only be heard where the 'sky-waves' came down to earth again, perhaps a hundred miles away. These might be picked up by stations in Germany, Belgium or Italy. I do not vouch for the reliability of this information, but I used it in organizing the security of my operator.

In the case of Honoré, for instance, I have already mentioned that we brought *two* sets with us. These were installed in different parts of Troyes.

At the first opportunity I had H.Q. drop me two more sets which were hidden with safe recruits in different places in the country each about twenty miles away (as I hoped, outside the range of the mysterious 'ground-wave').

Honoré, when D/F vans were reported, would ride about on his bicycle, taking one 'sked' here and the next one there, carrying only the precious crystals concealed on his person.

I remember that on one occasion we were racing towards a small village called Dierrey-Saint-Julien in great fear of arriving late for the 'sked'. One of the sets was in the custody of Madame Bourgeois who kept the local café and grocer's shop. We arrived just two minutes before time, the set was unearthed and opened up in a first-floor bedroom. The aerial wire was flung over the top of a great wardrobe and then Honoré asked, 'What about the earth connection?' I looked round. There was no running water in the house, and therefore no plumbing.

I espied a massive night-table beside the bed. I opened the door and, sure enough, inside was a monumental chamber-pot. I filled it from the water-jug, dropped the earth wire into it and told Honoré to get on with the job. He started, made contact immediately and the 'sked' was over, messages sent and received in a record short time at full strength.

Personally, I do not think the set really needed an earth connection at all, but that chamber-pot earned me the reputation of an electronics expert!

.   .   .   .   .

Dropping-grounds were quickly found and our first delivery was due. The B.B.C. message had come through, I had enjoyed the excitement of the novices and the evening ride, and while we were waiting in the moonlight I was giving the usual low-voiced explanations. The team—rather mixed as usual—consisted of Pierre Mulsant, Robert Stein (his brother-in-law), Balthazar (the driver who had transported Honoré's wireless equipment), Balthazar's future son-in-law and myself. Our vigil had been enlivened by a huge wild boar racing across the field. Pierre said it was a 'solitaire', a big fierce one and that if it came back and charged us we had better get out of the way.

At long last the plane was heard and the team ordered to their posts with the admonition to count the parachutes. By now the pattern of lights had been changed from a triangle to three lamps in a row at 100-yard intervals. The Halifax appeared out of the dark, swept overhead, circled and the cluster of parachutes burst forth. I counted them as they floated down to earth. It seemed to me there was one less than the expected number. After the usual rush towards the containers and the extra 'good-night' circle by the Halifax, I questioned the members of the team. They had all arrived at the same figure as myself.

We spent the rest of the night handling the stuff and next

morning it was carried to a temporary depot near Estissac. Pierre and I made an inventory and I found that some special supplies I had asked for were missing. Then we received a report that the Germans had arrested some people several miles away from the dropping-ground because 'they had received some arms dropped by parachute from an aeroplane'.

When I returned to Troyes I had Honoré send a message complaining that we were one container short. London later replied that the consignment was complete and that I must have lost one. I was sure that this was not so—also, there was this queer tale about the perfectly innocent people who had been in trouble with the Germans.

Long afterwards, when I was back in England, an R.A.F. officer who was concerned with our operations explained what had happened: while engaged on one of our operations, a bomber was nearing the target when the rear-gunner called over the intercom that one parachute had fallen away. The plane flew on, found the ground-signals, and the bomb-aimer pressed the switches and dropped the load of containers right over the lights.

A few days later, however, they heard that an agent thought he had been 'short changed'.

The R.A.F. engineers therefore tested that particular aircraft on the ground and in flight and found that, due to a defect in one of the electrical leads, there was a short circuit which set one container *adrift as soon as the bomb-doors were opened,* which was miles before the plane reached our ground. That explained it. The stray had been found by some inquisitive but innocent people and the Germans thought *they* must have been holding a reception committee!

What made me really sore was that, as fate would have it, it was precisely this stray which contained, among other things, the cigarettes, chocolate and other comforts for which I would have traded a few dozen hand-grenades any day!

.   .   .   .   .

Like all my fellow-agents, I had occasionally to cope with escaping airmen. In fact we had been meeting with them since early 1942, and, as our bombing increased, the number of aircraft shot down over Belgium, Holland and France grew. Many of those who reached the ground uninjured escaped the German patrols and were hidden by French country-people.

Among the several secret organizations at work in France was the Royal Air Force escape network.

This section, like our own, must have suffered many ups and downs, for on several occasions, when I had escaping airmen on my hands and radioed London for a contact to send them off, the reply was that, at the moment, the escape routes were blown and I would either have to keep them or find a way myself.

Nevertheless, airmen were trickling down to the Spanish frontier and getting across it.

A bomber would be hit by flak, the survivors among the crew would bale out, several would be caught by German patrols but one or two would get away to a farmhouse. The farmer might happen to know somebody who was working for the Resistance, and who would come and take them away. In other cases he would enquire from people he could trust and after a while make a connection.

The escapers would be provided with civilian clothing and passed from town to town, generally with guides for each part of the journey. At one of the stages they would be given false identity cards. And so, whether they happened to fall in with a 'regular' escape organization, with a special agent like myself, or merely friendly French people who spontaneously arranged for acquaintances and relatives to help them all along the route, they could, with luck, hope to reach the Spanish frontier zone, where a smuggler would get them across.

Once in Spain most of them were caught by the carabiñeros and taken to a jail or concentration camp such as Miranda. The British Consul would be advised and sooner or later, their bona fide as R.A.F. personnel having been established, they would be released for transfer to Gibraltar.

The R.A.F. men whom I saw after they had happened to be 'recuperated' by some of my own people were generally not quite unprepared for escaping. Before leaving England they had been given a little French money, a map in the form of a silk handkerchief, a cunning trouser-button which could serve as a tiny compass and a few other 'aids to navigation'. Some even had names and addresses of French people to whom they could apply if they crashed in a particular area.

I have never asked whether such names and addresses were supplied by the R.A.F. or privately by brother-airmen who had already been through the process.

Not all the escapers had to go through Spain. Some were exfiltrated by boat. Once I arranged for an airman to be flown back home by a Lysander 'pick-up' operation. This was against the rules, as *we* were not supposed to use our own devices for other purposes than our work.

In fact the official attitude was that we should never risk the security of our circuits by handling escapers. However, no special agent would turn one away. Some of my brother-agents even handled so many that they built up quite a large 'side-line' in this respect. After all, the R.A.F. were our particular friends, our transport and our R.A.S.C. When some of the boys in light-blue were in trouble, we felt we were in honour bound to help them if we could.

For instance, Johnny, the young sergeant who went home by Lysander, was a special case. He was in an aircraft which, when returning not from a bombing raid but from dropping containers in the east of France, was hit by flak and made a belly-landing.

He had hidden in a cornfield and not been found when the German patrols reached the wreckage. He later crawled to a farmhouse but the farmers were unable to shelter him for long. One of them knew of me and passed him on to one of my boys. London could give me no contact with an escape route just then, so I considered that as this man was engaged on dropping operations he was a kind of 'distant cousin', and at least knew that there

L

was some funny business going on, it would do no harm if he saw a bit more. Therefore I finally got him a seat in a Lysander and he was delivered to Tangmere aerodrome.

In addition to R.A.F. personnel, there had been Army escapers from the Saint-Nazaire and Dieppe raids, who had much the same experiences. Earlier still, in 1940, there had been escapers from the Dunkirk area. While I was in Madrid in 1942 I was told the story of the 'best soldier in the world'. He was a young private who had been left behind at Dunkirk and set off southwards apparently marching by night and hiding to sleep by day. After a considerable time he turned up *still in uniform* at the *British Embassy in Madrid*. Under his arm he was carrying a parcel wrapped in a newspaper, which, when opened, was found to contain, of all things, his tin hat!

When the Embassy officials asked him why on earth he had encumbered himself with such an object he replied that, while doing his training, the sergeant had told him of all the dreadful things that would be done to him if he lost that —— helmet!

Needless to say, the Germans used to try to penetrate the escape routes, and they sometimes succeeded. As I have shown, escapers used to come into contact with all kinds of resistance workers and agents, so that apart from the aspect of capturing escaping Service personnel there was the chance of discovering all kinds of subversive organizations. One of the ruses consisted in English-speaking Gestapo agents pretending to be shot-down airmen.

They would be dressed in uniforms and provided with papers, escape equipment, etc., taken from captured R.A.F. officers. They had to be able to speak English perfectly and to be familiar enough with England and the R.A.F. to pass the test of conversation. These bogus escapers would try to go through the whole process of asking for help at a farmhouse, being taken in charge by trusting patriots, and accomplishing the entire 'underground' journey, and thus obtain a wealth of information which could lead to the capture of a considerable number of patriots and agents. It was therefore necessary that escapers be examined rather carefully.

There were questions about their home town, bomber station, aircraft, flying equipment and general procedure.

One good test consisted in asking them questions about cricket, as this has always remained a mystery to even the most agile Continental minds. If a man knew that a 'silly mid-off' was not a stupid Russian and that 'bowling a maiden over' had nothing to do with love-making, he was most probably what he claimed to be. Of course, a Pole would be excused from this 'test-match'.

As the escapers could not speak French fluently, their golden rule was to keep their mouths tightly shut in trains or anywhere in public. We thus grew to refer to them as 'mutes'! 'André is bringing two mutes tonight.'

As the war wore on we began to meet American fliers also. Once several Flying Fortresses were shot down over Troyes, and there was the very dickens of a game of hide and seek between the German patrols rushing towards the places where parachutes were falling and the country-people racing to get there first and spirit the aviators away into woods and houses. Reports kept coming in: 'George has got one—Gaston has three—there are two with Etienne . . . etc.'

During the following days my friends were dodging about all over the area in every kind of vehicle available, moving the fallen airmen from one place to another, until all those who could be found were tucked away in various safe houses to await the time to move out.

I learned later that several of these did get safely back to England.

I think that airmen who have been through the experience will be almost unanimous in declaring that the French people they met behaved splendidly in such cases. Not only did they hide the men, and help them to escape, but fed them with the very best food they could buy, beg or borrow. There was something very moving about the spontaneity with which people would come to the help of unlucky airmen. They would even risk their lives to place flowers on the graves of those who had been found dead and buried by the enemy. The Germans did forbid any such marks of sympathy.

Of course, many airmen who landed safely were later caught. Although they were wearing civilian clothing and bearing false identity papers, the Germans, once satisfied that they *were* escaping Servicemen, would treat them as prisoners of war from then onwards, but any civilian arrested for aiding the escapee was considered as a terrorist and could be shot.

While on the subject of airmen, it may be well to recall the attitude of the French to bombing by the Allies. These airmen, for whose rescue they would risk their lives, were frequently engaged on attacking targets in France, and performing the cruel duty of dropping bombs which often killed their fellow-country-men and women, and sometimes even little children.

It would have seemed natural if the civilian population had put all bomber crews, friend and foe, in the same bag and shown resentment or at least indifference to their fate.

But the patriotic section of the population did not feel this way.

In a country with a long military tradition, whenever a group of people were mourning the victims of a bombardment or deploring the damage done, there would nearly always be a voice raised to remind them of the grim necessities of war. For many this apocalyptic warfare was too vast to be measured by normal human standards, and they eventually ceased to connect individual airmen with the smoking ruins.

14. Noisy nights

IN TROYES I soon came into contact with one of the big French resistance organizations which were in touch with the B.C.R.A. in London. This occurred when some members of the professional and business classes were sounded as possible recruits. In a town with a population of 50,000 it was natural that the feelings of the more prominent citizens should be known, and it was not surprising that several of them were approached by more than one 'firm'.

As usual, I found that of those who had already been enrolled by the French the more realistic men were quite eager to help my circuit, although this was discouraged by their chiefs in the other organization. The patriots concerned, however, had no patience with high-level bickerings. As I had my own radio-operator I was able to produce supplies and get things done quickly, without having to go through a chain of communications. In short, the principle of one organizer one W/T was beginning to pay off.

I met one of the most important local members of the O.C.M., Dr. Mahée.

He was a splendid man and his loyalty to his own organization was absolute. However, he could see no reason why I should not supply some of the groups under his control with the weapons and sabotage materials I was in a position to obtain. He helped me to establish myself and introduced me to local resistance workers.

He never asked any questions, never tried to find out where

Honoré worked, and actually supplied me with some furniture to set up house.

In return I exhibited no curiosity about his own activities.

I never mixed my own recruits with the 'other firm's'. My people in the area were, moreover, divided into two circuits which worked unknown to each other.

There is a tremendous amount of gossip in a provincial town of 50,000 souls and rumours fly fast. It was soon whispered among the resistance people and others that there was an English agent in the town. What was important was that the enemy should not learn who my contacts were; some of them, such as Pierre Mulsant, were well known in the town. If I alone were spotted I could hope to hide, but my recruits were tied to their houses, businesses, farms and families, and were very vulnerable.

When we had received some supplies and they had been duly delivered to an arms depot, I had quite a lot of bombs to make up.

The plastic explosive had to be kneaded into small cubes. In each was buried a conical piece of solid explosive called a primer. Through a hole in the primer was threaded a short length of silver-coloured detonating cord whose ends protruded from the cube so that detonators and time-pencils could be attached. The bomb was then wrapped in black cloth secured by adhesive tape.

The almond smell of plastic explosive permeated the empty house and I often thought that, working at the table in my shirt-sleeves, with piles of hand-grenades and incendiary pots, and rows of Sten-guns and pistols along the walls, I must have looked the almost perfect picture of an anarchist preparing to blow up the Grand Duke of Moldavo-Slavonia in a pre-1914 theatre play. I only needed a pair of false whiskers.

The charges, when made up, had to be distributed to our various customers. For obvious security reasons I did not want a constant stream of visitors to my arms depot. Only two or three assistants knew where it was. This meant quite a lot of cycling, sometimes towing a trailer. Occasionally the goods would be delivered by motor-car.

Unfortunately, there were frequent searches on the roads by

the Feldgendarmes, who also enforced traffic regulations. For instance, cyclists were not allowed to ride two or more abreast. The Feldgendarmes would sometimes watch from the top of a hill through field-glasses. When they espied a couple of offenders approaching they would halt and fine them on the spot. They were also as strict about bicycles with no rear light as the present-day road-police ought to be.

Once I was pedalling a set of railway charges when two Feldgendarmes popped out of a bush, one of them raising the stick with the red disc on the end which they used as a stop signal. I jammed the brakes on so hard that the wheels locked and skidded as I hopped off ready for trouble, but the stick was lowered, the helmets nodded and the two stood aside and waved me along.

I remounted and when I had gone a short distance turned round in the saddle to look backwards. I saw the two stop another cyclist, make him get off, seize the handlebars, start pushing the bike forward, and obviously begin remonstrating with the rider.

They were merely testing the brakes of all bicycles! Good for them!

On another occasion I was riding through the town taking a 'one-night's outfit' to a good client. It was contained in a cheap imitation-patent-leather shopping-bag slung from the handlebars. Right in the middle of the busiest street I suddenly saw that the wretched bag had split and that some loose ends of detonating cord and the muzzle of a heavy-calibre automatic pistol were hanging out for all to see. I put a hand into the bag and quickly pulled them in.

Another time Pierre was quite elated when he returned from a similar errand. He had been riding a light low-built motor-cycle and was stopped by a patrol who searched the case which was strapped on to the luggage-carrier over the back wheel, while Pierre remained in the saddle. They found nothing and let him go. Actually the explosives and weapons were in a parcel which he had placed in front of the saddle, on the top of the streamlined petrol-tank and between his long legs, where it was covered by the billowing folds of a very loose raincoat he was wearing. He said he had only put it there by chance but it was a good trick to remember.

When bigger loads had to be moved we took a motor-lorry and sometimes used the device which, I feel sure, was discovered sooner or later by each and every agent in the field—the lorry was a charcoal burner, but a little petrol could be obtained and the engine run on that. The great unused generator-cylinder by the side of the cab could then be filled with stuff. With a bit of research into combustion engineering it was even possible to make smoke come out to complete the illusion of a fire within!

Now and then both Honoré and I needed a few hours' relaxation and we had an ideal place to go to.

We would mount our bicycles and pay a visit to Madame Mielle—a remarkable lady who owned a country restaurant in a picture-book hamlet called Précy-Notre-Dame, about twenty miles from Troyes. Madame Mielle was simply the best cook in the world and a well-known figure, but for a long time no one suspected that she was a member of our circuit. She was later to do very valuable work for which she was awarded the M.B.E.

As I have already said, it was very important in long-term work to have some totally independent and alternative contacts and safe houses. It was best not only to refrain from putting all your eggs in one basket, but to have some spare baskets as well. Speaking of eggs, Madame Mielle also provided us with plenty of food to take home.

But let us get back to our explosives.

For Whom the Bell Tolls is a very fine film which has been enjoyed by many. Towards the end of the war I went to see it in the company of a close friend. As we left the cinema he commented: 'It was very good, but what a fuss over blowing up a small bridge! All that scheming, all those intrigues, why didn't he get on with the job right at the beginning?—But, of course, there would then have been no film and no Ingrid Bergman!'

I retorted, 'My lad, strange as it may seem, it often was like that, going round in circles for days, even when there was no pretty girl mixed up in it.'

To illustrate this, here is the story of a small 'bang':

Some of the acts of sabotage which were carried out during the war (and afterwards by the Jews in Palestine, for instance) were tremendous operations both by their effects and the incredible daring of their perpetrators.

I am afraid that such jobs as Norwegian heavy water-plants and Israeli roly-poly bombs either did not come my way or else I got out of theirs (preferably by proclaiming them impossible). By comparison, in the days I am writing of, the sneak hole-and-corner nuisance or large-scale practical joke was the order of the day.

At Troyes there was a very important locomotive depot. It had two roundhouses, looking like giant circular stables, where engines are parked like the spokes of a wheel, the hub of which is a great turntable. When an engine is taken home it is driven along a track which leads into the roundhouse and on to the turntable, and is then swung round until it is pointing towards a vacant 'stall', into which it is backed. Incidentally, one good method of causing momentary trouble is to jam the turntable, as the engines then cannot get out. Our Headquarters, however, wanted more durable results and it was decided to attack the locomotives themselves.

First of all a look at the job was necessary. As card-players have been known to claim, 'a little peep is better than a great deal of deduction'. Dr. Mahée, in whom I confided, introduced me to a railway official, M. Thierry, who took me to visit the railway football-ground which was near the depot. I was supposed to be the manager of a rival team having a look at the field with a view to fixing a game. What was more natural then that he should afterwards take me over to see the roundhouses? They were about 100 yards in diameter and certainly impressive. As we wandered about in the great caverns he pointed out the most valuable types of engines and then led me out by the route he recommended for entry by night. This was through a lean-to which contained an old locomotive boiler being used as a steam generator. It had two doors, one to the roundhouse (fortunately the one which contained the best engines), another to the yard. From there along the lines and down a cinder-track to a wicket-gate on a small road which led under a bridge. Just opposite the wicket-gate was a house occupied by Germans, but my friend said that engine crews frequently came and went at night without being challenged. The armed sentries would be in the yards and inside the roundhouses. It appeared then that by getting in via the steam boiler it should be possible to creep along the wall and get under the locomotives without being seen from the turntable.

I now had to settle the details.

The timing of the operation would directly determine the number of men required. I decided that the team should spend not more than one hour inside the roundhouse, so that the men would have time to get home long before daybreak although the summer nights were short. I also had to determine how long it would take to doctor each engine. Of course, practical advice had been given in England, but there is nothing like finding out for yourself. This meant a nocturnal visit on my own, so I would be able to tell an inexperienced team exactly what to do. After all, they would be risking their lives and would therefore be entitled to accurate directions.

The next few days were spent trying to find three men, which seemed the right number. This search had the inevitable effect of noising the business abroad and I heard several bits of advice. I was told that the job had been contemplated before but found to be impossible as the night guard was too strong.

So, one evening, I donned a suit of blue overalls and rubber-soled gym shoes and set forth from my arms depot which was about two miles from the target. My route led down back alleys and lanes to a little road which crossed the railway lines outside the town. There I found a first obstacle: a strong lamp brightly illuminating the level-crossing.

I waited in the dark until a couple of other overalled figures appeared making for the crossing. I tagged along behind and got over into the dark on the other side. I found my way to the wicket-gate and pushed it open without looking towards the

German post behind me. Up the cinder-track, along the lines and into the boiler-house. In the pitch darkness I felt my way around the hissing bulk and slipped through into the roundhouse, behind the tender of a parked locomotive. I dived down into the pit under the engine and crawled under the axles to look out under the front wheels. The turntable was illuminated and a number of men, including guards, were there chatting. I began to feel for a suitable place to wedge the explosive charge. It was rather difficult to find and I was glad I had come to explore. After about fifteen minutes I discovered a good spot and mentally located it by feeling its position in relation to the piston-rods and stuffing-boxes.

I then slipped out from under the first engine and went under a couple of others of different types to study the particular anatomy of each.

After about an hour, during which I had become quite used to the guards passing a few feet away on the outside of the wheels, I withdrew the way I had come and walked out confidently through the wicket-gate and under the light at the level-crossing.

I was almost able to find my way back by the different sounds of the snorings I had noted and catalogued coming through the open windows on my way out.

Well, it appeared M. Thierry had been quite right. It was a piece of cake, albeit a dirty cake, as I was coated with dirt and grease.

The next day I went to visit the doctor and said the job could be done without much trouble. He was very pleased but asked whether I would mind taking *five* men with me, instead of two or three, as it would be good training for them to do their first job under 'expert leadership'. (Bows and blushes by yours truly.)

I was later introduced to the first man, Senée. He was young, calm and efficient and it was arranged that we should meet the others in a few days.

The doctor, however, began to appear worried. There seemed to be trouble with his organization. There had been a few arrests and he feared some indiscretions had been committed. He loyally warned me that he himself might be suspect and that I should be careful. He would not go into hiding as a precaution. It might attract attention and discourage his men.

I well remember the fine, warm evening when he told me of his anxieties. We were in the tastefully furnished drawing-room on the first floor of his house. There was a charming old spinet in one corner. In the dusk the open windows afforded a view of one of the magnificent ancient churches of which there are several in Troyes, the 'ville sonnante' as Rabelais called it. In this exquisite setting this cultured man was calmly weighing the fate in store for him. His voice was sad, but there was no alarm in it.

This was a situation typical of the Resistance: the comfortable home into which the Gestapo might burst any hour, the atmosphere of the invisible web being spun, the feeling that any chances of allaying suspicions would be dashed by the sudden flight of a well-known citizen, and that the best thing was to stay and, if necessary, try to brazen it out. Once again I felt my own invulnerability compared to the local people.

Actually the blow fell quickly. A few days later the townspeople noticed a number of German cars driving about in all directions and apparently being used for driving lessons. Each car carried several soldiers and would stop now and then so that each man could take the wheel in turn. That night a considerable number of houses were suddenly surrounded and a big arresting operation was carried out. Dr. Mahée was among the captives. That driving school had been merely a cover for driving the feldpolitzei through the town so they might have a good look at the premises they were to raid.

First reports indicated that none of my own people were in trouble, but the same old question arose: how much did the arrested persons know about us? After a couple of days it was possible to take stock. The French organization was badly damaged but there were a number of members left who had apparently not yet been suspected. M. Thierry was one of these.

None of my own people seemed to be in trouble. The doctor had obviously not let out a single word, in spite of what he must have been going through.

Well, it was no use crying over spilt milk and the locomotive depot still needed attending to. Senée got the team together and I was waiting for a moonless night. Thierry informed me that in one of the roundhouses there was a batch of brand-new big express locomotives which had been commandeered by the Germans. Then Pierre Mulsant received through his grapevine a report that the Germans had learned that sabotage of the engine depot was being planned. This was certainly a snag, and I felt sore at having probably got thoroughly dirty for nothing. I put it to the men. They took the attitude: 'Damn the Gestapo, who do they think they are, anyway?' Then Thierry came with the good news that, when backing into its stall, an engine had overrun and smashed a great gap in the outer wall. This seemed to be an omen beckoning us on. I decided we would get in through that very hole.

.   .   .   .   .

One of the sabotage team was a schoolmaster and the briefing was held in the schoolroom one evening. The hefty saboteurs were sitting like good little boys at the low desks. I had issued each man with a set of bombs and accessories, an automatic pistol, and a complimentary ration of cigarettes and chocolate.

I gave my little lecture standing at the blackboard and making chalk drawings of the layout of the roundhouse, with the supposed positions of the guards, the method of entry and withdrawal, the exact locations for the charges, etc. I then explained how the time-pencils and detonators should be used and answered a number of questions. We decided on the rendezvous for the night of the operation and finally went home. Next morning I suddenly remembered that I had forgotten to wipe the blackboard and that the drawings with the unmistakable outline of the target and the plan of the attack had been left for the schoolchildren or anyone else to see! What a clot! Luckily no harm was done. The school-master's wife had seen the blackboard in time and wiped it clean of its unholy lesson before the children arrived.

.   .   .   .   .

The rendezvous was at midnight under a small bridge which spanned the canal, not far from the railway. We were divided into three pairs. I took Senée with me. He came to my arms depot in the evening and we waited for pitch blackness before setting out.

We each carried a small rucksack containing the made-up charges and a pistol. I led the way through the same back alleys and lanes I had followed during my reconnaissance. We had not gone far when we suddenly found ourselves faced by two German sentries on patrol.

In the blackness we saw them only when it was too late to hide; they were about twenty yards away. They stopped in the lane and watched us. Senée and I kept on towards them mutter-ing: We may have to kill these two.—Yes, but the noise may mean abandoning the job.—Looks as if they *are* expecting some-thing.—Well, here goes, let us start talking about fishing.—Is your safety-catch off? Then in a louder voice: Do you really believe the fish do rise at night?—Of course, I promised you a good fry.—I'll believe it when I taste it. (Of course, we had no reason to believe these Germans could understand French.)

The sentries stood stock-still as we bore down on them. They had every reason to challenge us. It was after curfew and we both had bags and were wearing overalls; but was it some mysterious telepathy which gave an indefinable warning in their sub-conscious mind? Some animal voice which in the dark of night whispered to them: 'These two men approaching are your death; it is much safer to assume they are just harmless chaps; your officer is not here, why bother? . . .' Be that as it may, they remained still and staring as we walked past only a few feet away. We did not look back until we were sure we were lost in the dark.

I was wearing my rubber-soled gym shoes, but Senée had his boots on, and his tramping sounded loud in the night, so I told him to take them off and the poor chap spent all the rest of the night wearing great holes in his socks. However, our progress became noiseless.

As we approached the level-crossing there was a pleasant surprise—the bright light was out! With a sigh of relief we slunk over the lines and went on our way to the canal. We slipped down to the bank and, under the little bridge, there were the four others who had come from the town side. There was some time to wait and in whispers we went over the arrangements. Each man had his little bag of mischief. They were in high spirits and were fondling their pistols. I really believe they were itching for a fight and almost hoping for some opposition, so I insisted that this was a respectable firm and that they were only to fire in self-defence and at close range. (My own practice had led me to believe that, fired by the average person, a pistol would merely be a useless noise at a range of more than a dozen yards!)

Zero hour came and we moved out. No more talking now. We got to the deserted road, crossed over and went up the path to the wicket-gate. There seemed to be a bit of shouting a short distance away in the marshalling-yard, but no sign of life in the Germans' house.

We marched in single file up the cinder-track and saw in the side of the roundhouse the gaping hole which was shown up by the dim glow from the light over the turntable within.

A few seconds later we filed inside behind the tender of the nearest engine and all crawled underneath.

I felt my way towards the front and began to paw at the cylinder ends. The others pressed around me as I guided their hands to the right spot. The guards in the middle were in full view between the front bogie-wheels. Their voices, as they chatted, echoed under the great vaulted roof. I spotted one of my men hungrily taking a bead with his pistol and pushed it down: None of that!—Oh, but it would be so easy!—Not unless you have to, I say!

The first pair were left under that engine, with instructions to fix it and its neighbours.

The rest moved around to two different sectors. Each pair would attend to five or six locomotives.

Senée and I doctored three or four engines and then went outside again to attend to some more which were standing on sidings. M. Thierry had been careful to tell me which were the most valuable types.

When the prearranged time for withdrawal came we still had some charges left but could not stay as the time-pencils chosen had a sixty-minute delay and we wanted everybody out before the fireworks started. Admitting the first ones had been pressed about fifteen or twenty minutes after our entry, we had just enough time to get away.

We had not gone far beyond the level-crossing when a great boom rang out through the night. 'There goes the first one!' Then, almost immediately, or so it seemed, we heard the noise of a German motor-cycle. There was no mistaking the deep sound of the powerful twin-cylinder engine. Other motors opened up and it was as if a beehive had been aroused.

—So they *were* on the alert, after all!

—Yes, funny we were able to do it.

—But, come on, we had better take to the fields.

We got off the road and sprinted around a small farmhouse. Suddenly I was stopped dead, flattened against an invisible wall. I felt just like one of Walt Disney's characters which is arrested suddenly in the midst of a great leap in mid-air. My face must have worn the same surprised look as Pluto or Donald Duck! And there, by my side, was Senée spread-eagled just as I was. Well, of course, we might have expected that a farmhouse would have a hen-coop surrounded by chicken-wire! We felt our way around the invisible obstruction and decided there was no sense in running after all.

We were relieved to get back to the arms depot where Senée could put up his poor feet. The explosions were occurring at intervals. We avoided making a light and attracting attention while we tried to clean ourselves of the grease and dirt. The sparsely furnished house had no bed, but we were too tense to sleep. We sat up in the darkness waiting for daylight. Morning came and, at a respectable hour, Senée went home.

I stayed on until Pierre Mulsant's driver, Balthazar, came and brought me some food, as I had asked him to. He had listened to the bangs and told me that the din had been heard all over the town.

Later on, having cleaned up, I got on my bicycle, and rode out to Précy-Notre-Dame, to lunch at Madame Mielle's. I felt a need to relax. In one corner of the charming little dining-room sat Professor Langevin, the well-known physicist, who, because of his Communist sympathies, was confined to that area.

During the meal a man arrived from Troyes and excitedly gave the news: the 'rotondes' had been attacked and thirteen locomotives were beyond repair—the job must have been done by a 'specialist' who had put bombs 'in the cylinders'. Nobody had been hurt, and the saboteurs had not been caught or even seen. Every time someone entered the room, he told his story all over again. Was that a twinkle in the Professor's eye? Of course we had not been introduced, but he was a good friend of Madame Mielle's . . . so I wondered. . . .

When I returned to town I began to receive reports from various sources. The figure of thirteen was correct. We had been able to get in and out as the result of an amazing bit of luck: a few minutes before our zero hour a goods-waggon had derailed in the marshalling-yard. That was why we heard shouting in that direction. The Germans *had* been expecting an attack, but, having arrested a lot of people a few days before, were convinced they had decapitated the local resistance and were probably holding the would-be saboteurs.

When the waggon was derailed they thought this must be a small job performed by a few survivors. The extra guards had therefore gone to look.

When, a short while later, the first explosion occurred in the roundhouse, the guards inside had had the fright of their life.

M

What a bang it must have made inside that huge structure! The others rushed in to investigate and try to catch the culprit. Then the second charge detonated. . . . Exit everybody amid the glass falling from the roof. Realizing there might be more to come they threw a cordon around the building and listened to the successive explosions.

Then the reinforcements had begun to arrive in cars and trucks. The commandant himself turned up and began to bawl out his men. He is said to have climbed on to the footplate of one of the engines on the sidings outside, the better to gesticulate. Alas! this was one of those Senée and I had fixed before we left. The charge went off just then and the commandant jumped off and fell to the ground on the seat of his pants.

When daylight came it appeared that there were to be no more bangs, a few of the French railwaymen were detained and the Germans gingerly went in to investigate. While assessing the damage they found a charge which had failed to explode. Their specialists pronounced it to be made in strict accordance with the British pattern and declared that it must be an outside professional job. The Frenchmen were released forthwith.

The business had an amusing sequel: the next day the Germans began to erect wooden barriers on the pavements in front of their establishments. And to whom did they apply for materials: Pierre Mulsant! The German officer who came to place the order said: 'Ah, yes! . . . There are still terrorists left in Troyes; there must certainly be an Englishman among them. All this is bad for Franco-German relations.'

Pierre charged a good price for the wood and when he reported the interview offered me a German cigarette . . . he had picked the German officer's pocket in the bargain! It was one of those little finishing touches which give such pleasure.

This was a modest operation and would probably not have succeeded without the coincidence of the purely accidental derailment in the marshalling-yard. Needless to say, no one would believe that I was not responsible for this diversion! It went off perfectly, however; there were no casualties among the saboteurs;

and the 'signature' provided by the charge which failed to explode avoided the arrest of innocent men. The French were delighted. Even the unhappy prisoners who were lying in the town jail were aroused by the noise, and able to count the successive explosions as they thundered through the stillness of the night.

Coming on the heels of what they had believed to have been the 'clean-up' of the area, the attack gave the Germans a shaking.

In the main, and apart from a few blunders, the operation had followed the pattern which was being taught in the special training schools in England, and for this reason was later deemed interesting by our headquarters in London.

For Thierry this was but a beginning. He was later to organize attacks on dozens and dozens of locomotives at various depots, depriving the Germans of desperately needed motive power.

Lastly, my friends were much entertained during the following weeks listening to people who could tell just how it had been done, some even claiming to have partaken in it. According to one of the stories which was going about, a squad of British sappers had been dropped from an aeroplane near the railway yards, and picked up later by the same machine which had landed in a field. Pierre would come and say, 'I have just been talking to yet another chap who did it; this one got in through the roof. . . .'

15. Friends in trouble

ALL over France members of the Resistance movement were going about their work, picking their way through traps and ambushes and surviving careless gossip by their friends.

On the radio there were more and more personal messages, indicating a growing number of dropping operations all over the country. Not all were successful, unfortunately. The Germans were capturing many of the deliveries. Through treason or indiscretion they had advance intelligence of some of the operations and laid ambushes.

Some of the aircraft were shot down on the way.

I heard of supplies being lost because the size and weight of the containers had not been properly impressed on the inexperienced reception committee and the number of men sent to the dropping-ground was too small to handle the whole delivery, a large part of which had to be abandoned.

In the summer the weather was fine but the nights were short. In the winter the nights were long but the sky was often overcast, so careful planning by the R.A.F. was required all the year round.

One day a visitor arrived from Paris. He was a man named Octave Simon, a brilliant sculptor, who had dedicated himself, body and soul, to the Resistance work.

He had come to tell me that Prosper and many others of his circuit had just been arrested. There had been a sudden wave of almost simultaneous arrests, and our losses were heavy.

Prosper, his radio-operator Archambaud, another agent named Sebastien, the latter's radio-operator Achilles, several other

agents in various parts of the country, a number of their recruits—
the dreadful list grew. It was a catastrophe. Our friend Gary, alias
'Cinema', seemed to be safe and was still able to get through to
London, thanks to a young girl radio-operator who had arrived
in Paris and was in his care—her operational name was Nurse (she
was actually named Inayat Khan)—but it was difficult to know
where the dry-rot would stop. I wrote the message of bad tidings
and Honoré sent it out that same day. It crossed a brief incoming
message from London saying, 'Break immediately all contacts
with Prosper circuit.' They had evidently received news from
some other source also and were warning all agents.

As the tale unfolded it began to take on a familiar pattern. I
had seen this kind of thing before.

There had been the arrival of several agents. The creation of
circuits by each. The expansion. The establishment of contacts
between circuits, sometimes developing into an amalgamation
which led to some junior recruits each knowing several organizers and their radio-operators. This association of efforts
made work a lot easier but often meant sacrificing long-term
security to immediate convenience. Such a state of affairs was by
no means entirely the fault of the men in the field.

London would frequently send agents to the care of a well-
established organizer such as Prosper and the newcomers would
turn out to have tongues which wagged at both ends, unquench-
able thirsts, or unbounded admiration for ladies. The result would
be that soon strange people would begin to turn up at various
accommodation addresses, with recommendations from some
garrulous busybody, and the organizer would be horrified to see
how much they already knew.

And so, as the organization expanded, much good work
would be done, many tons of weapons and explosives would be
received, but at the same time, as more and more people were
enrolled, the whole network would become more and more
vulnerable.

The old adage that imparting a secret to one person is equivalent to telling ten is descriptive of our 'occupational disease'.

Thus the risk of 'contamination' grew rapidly. A small leak would attract the enemy's attention to a first suspect, he would be followed and, realizing they were perhaps on the track of a subversive network, they would put more and more counterespionage men on the job, trying, if possible, to penetrate it and discover the leader. When it was decided the fruit was ripe, the arrests would be made, and with the intercommunication between circuits new trails might be discovered which led to heretofore unsuspected groups.

It should be almost possible for a mathematician to devise an equation which would give the probable length of life of a network in function of the number of members and quantity of supplies received. I think this hypothetical formula would give an average expectation of circuit-life of five or six months. When a circuit blew up the casualty rate among the local French recruits was high. There would be some sad cases of people being brutally hauled off to jail and beaten up only a few days after they had joined.

A number of our agents were dropped to 'blown' circuits and collared as soon as they arrived.

I had at least a run for my money through luck and excessive caution.

I have mentioned that suicide was suggested as a remedy in case of capture. Most of us did not consider it seriously, but some did actually use it. There were men—and what men!—who, either at the moment of arrest, or after having withstood several 'interrogations', decided to suppress the possibility of their flesh influencing their moral fibre and to kill themselves by whatever means were available—swallowing the pill if they still had it, jumping out of a high window if one was handy, cutting an artery if they could manage to conceal a piece of sharp metal or glass. I know an officer who was captured and escaped death by a miracle. His wrists still bear scars to show that for a whole night he cut and dug with a tiny piece of tin which proved just a bit too short, in an attempt to give his friends the supreme protection. We must all die, but I have always thought it must have been hard to kill oneself all alone in a foul, smelly dungeon when one had every faith in forthcoming victory.

When a network had been blown a disagreeable task had often to be performed—visiting premises which had just been raided to see whether some confidential material could be retrieved or whether the Gestapo had found it.

There was always the possibility of a 'mousetrap' having been set up, and it was better to risk it only when absolutely necessary. The scene must be familiar to many resistance workers. The first move was a walk down the street past the door and around the block. If no doubtful characters were to be seen and no motor-cars (usually Citroëns with front-wheel drive which the Gestapo favoured) found standing in the immediate neighbourhood, the investigator would enter the building. A glance in the direction of the concierge's *loge* would generally reveal that lady peering, motionless, through the traditional lace curtains of the glass door, and apparently alone.

Up the stairs and on to the landing opposite the raided flat. A minute or so spent in listening, then press the button and also knock, in case the bell is not working. After a short while there is a sound of tiptoeing footsteps, which pause on the other side of the door. If there are two flats on the same landing the investigator goes and stands at the other door. In such circumstances the mind clutches at the smallest hope. If the first bursts open and reveals two men with raised guns perhaps a blank look and such a remark as, 'Oh, sorry, I rang first at your door by mistake,' or, 'Hey, don't make any mistakes it was another fellow who rang your bell and he has just run off downstairs again,' may save the uneasy caller. What a hope!

However, the door opens slowly and a woman's pale face peers round the edge.

She opens it a bit further to let the caller into the dark corridor, closes it gently behind him and moves softly to the door of the dining-room, as if admitting a visitor into a house where a dead person is lying. She has been crying.

A whispered conversation ensues: 'What happened?'—'Oh,

you should not have come—they were here and took him—they are sure to be back!'—'Did they search the flat?'—'Yes, but not very thoroughly—I was in the bedroom when they came—Mother opened the door—they said "Police Allemande" and pushed their way in—saw him in the dining-room and went after him—I got the papers, slipped into the kitchen and pushed them in the stove. They handcuffed him and made him sit on a chair while they had a quick look round—they opened a few drawers, and then they took him away—they told Mother and me to stay here—I slipped down to the concierge—they had told her they were coming back and that in the meantime she was to ring a number they gave her if we had any callers. She will not, of course, but I am sure they will return.'

'I am sure too—you and your mother had better clear out at once—come with me!'—'Mother does not want to leave!' An old lady appears at the door, 'No, I am old—I have lived here so long —they cannot do much to me—but you must go.'—'No, Mother, I won't leave you—after all they may not want us—he will tell them we know nothing!' The poor old lady looks grey and drawn. 'My poor son . . . my little boy!' The investigator insists: 'Come away—you can take no chances with those people—they will be checking his identity—as soon as they are sure he is the man who has been denounced to them and that they are on the right track they will be back here to set up a mousetrap and arrest everybody who calls and you will be taken too!'

'No, I cannot—the only chance for my son is that they may think we have nothing to hide, whereas if they find us gone it will go harder with him.'

'Madame, I beg of you . . .'—'No, monsieur—but you—you must not stay here—you are young—you can go on and avenge him!'

In the two women's eyes is the familiar hunted look—the wide-open eyelids—the dark, staring pupils.

The clock is ticking away. A detail may be at this moment receiving their instructions to rush back here and set up the mousetrap.

The women will not come. The investigator will only destroy any chance they may have of being left alone if he is found here, to say nothing of his being taken himself. The latter possibility assumes enormous importance.

He moves to the door. The younger woman opens it gently and they both listen. There is no sound on the staircase. He slips out and tiptoes down the stairs. He steps out into the hallway, past the concierge's *loge*. Her head appears again, indistinct through the lace curtains.

He goes out of the main door, his eyes scanning the street. There is nothing unusual in sight. He walks on to the first corner. He hears a car coming fast from behind. A sudden screeching of brakes and tyres as it is level with him. It is a German staff car. He holds his breath. The car accelerates round the corner without the occupants having even looked at him. So that was *not* it.

He walks on round several blocks until he is satisfied he is not being shadowed.

That old lady could have been one of several I have visited in similar circumstances. She could have been one of those who were arrested later the same day, deported, and who died at Ravensbruck.

As a result of all the arrests, the Germans obtained as usual some W/T transmitters and were trying to play them back. Sometimes they succeeded. Our H.Q. in London had to look out for anything doubtful in the messages. Each operator had security-checks he incorporated in the messages to establish their genuineness. If captured, he would appear to agree to operating for the Germans, but omit these security checks, and thus let H.Q. know he was a prisoner.

I incline to the view that the frequently garbled condition of the signals rendered such devices unreliable.

When in doubt the home station could put a personal question to the operator, which gave him a chance of deliberately sending a wrong answer to show he was in trouble.

Also, there was supposed to be a record of each man's 'key-touch', by which he could be recognized very much as by his step, but we had reason to be sceptical about this, as we were able to substitute operators without drawing comment from home.

Another device was introduced called 'S-phone'. It was a tiny low-powered radio-telephone transmitter which allowed conversation between a reception committee and the crew of the aircraft.

Its range was so short that detection was practically impossible.

A liaison officer could travel in the bomber to have a chat with an organizer while over the dropping-ground.

It could be very useful and it was fun . . . it was also another piece of equipment to be looked after.

On several dropping operations I found boxes of a most improbable substance—itching powder. I felt quite insulted at first. Did they think we were just naughty schoolboys? Then one day we enlisted a woman who worked in a laundry which was under contract for washing the underwear of the Wehrmacht. Oh, yes —she could use the itching powder! Students of the German language were much interested by some new and very fearful Teutonic oaths which were to be heard soon afterwards!

Among the recruits Pierre Mulsant and I used to see with great pleasure were a family of farmers named Buridant of Bar-sur-Aube. It was always good to visit them. There was a small dropping-ground in the nearby woods and the receptions were very much of a 'family affair'. The security was so good that this ground was used right up to the end of the occupation—in fact, it came to be referred to as *la gare* (the railway station) because it was such a reliable place of arrival from England! The men of the family used to play in the local brass band: who could look less suspicious to a German?

However, like all my brother-agents, I was unable to restrict my contacts to people whose security was beyond doubt.

It was necessary also to accept rendezvous with unfortunates who were survivors of 'blown' groups. On a fine, warm, sunny day in Paris I might have to meet such a man at a certain spot in a park. As I waited I could watch the children playing and bask in the unique Parisian atmosphere to which I have always been so sensitive. Then I would see my friend approaching under the trees. Was he 'contaminated'? Was he one of those who had been left free so that he would sooner or later unknowingly lead our enemies to just such a rendezvous as this? Had he made sure he was not being followed? How security-minded was he? I would find myself scanning the terrain, examining every person in view and trying to pick out every probable point of vantage from which a watcher could spy on us. As he drew near I would tell myself that there was probably no danger, but that it would be too silly to catch the disease this way. Then he would reach me and smile. We would saunter along together and engage in conversation. He would give me the news. For the last week he had been sleeping in a different place every night—so-and-so had been taken—somebody else wanted to see me, but I had better be careful as he thought his home was being watched, etc.

We would both stop talking as a man walked close by. No, he was probably just an ordinary pedestrian.

My friend had also heard that a message from one of our arrested agents had been brought out of jail. He was accusing a certain person of having betrayed him. I would ask after another friend—'Oh, yes! I was forgetting, he has been arrested too. Do you know, I saw him only the day before and *he had the look of one who is going to be taken.*' Yes, I understood, I knew that look—it was a curious thing, too curious to believe unless you had seen it.

Our business completed, we would part. I would walk some distance through open spaces and then round a few corners. No one was following. The sunshine was warm again. I would stop worrying and give myself up to the feeling which I suppose we all shared, 'It can't happen to me.' So back to business as usual. More bicycle rides, analysing reports on prospective recruits, contradictory information about the guarding of certain targets, belly-aching from Honoré because for several days he had been unable to make contact with the home station owing to bad 'sky conditions', etc.

No sketches of an agent's life would be complete without the story of a fright, so I will describe one of mine.

One morning I was returning on my bicycle from my arms depot when a motor-car coming in the opposite direction pulled in to the side of the road and the driver signalled me to stop. I recognized one of my own men. He told me my arms depot was 'blown'. A neighbour had written to the police saying there must be some queer goings-on in my place. He had given the number of Pierre's motor-car which he had once seen standing in front of the house. Luckily for us a patriotic French police-official had seen the denunciation before it reached the Germans; he had looked up the car's number, found out to whom it belonged and warned Pierre's father-in-law (this showed our 'intelligence' was good). Quick action was necessary. I got hold of Pierre—we had to get all the stuff away to somewhere else. It was not so much the loss of those supplies which would have been serious (there did not happen to be a great deal of stuff there anyway just then) as that their discovery would certainly have led to the arrest of the man who had provided the house. The licence number would put the Gestapo on Pierre's track, and all because of the stupidity of one wretched idiot who didn't even know what it was all about. Many resistance workers were captured through such stupidity. Therefore when the police raided the place they must find *absolutely nothing*. The whole affair could then probably be dismissed with a general shrugging of shoulders.

There was no time to lose. The first thing to do was find another place nearby to which the stuff could be taken. Pierre knew the right man—his name was Georges Avelines—he was a carpenter who had his own well-equipped workshop only a short distance from the arms depot. We asked him to hide our beastly supplies, warning him that the removal involved considerable risk as, for all we knew, our depot might be watched already. He grinned and said he would be delighted to help. A plan was hastily made. I did not want anyone in the street to see faces they might be able to name. They were welcome to have a look at my own gargoyle. I was only a 'fictitious' person anyway. Pierre and Georges wanted to go to the depot to clear it out, but I insisted on their keeping watch as I arrived at the workshop. If they sighted any suspicious-looking character, they would signal to me to pass by, without entering. We met at Georges's workshop. A trailer was attached behind my bicycle. I confess to drinking a litre of red wine. I set off on the first trip. As I rounded the corner I saw my street was empty and all was quiet. I left the trailer in the yard, went inside and began loading the stuff into sacks. I put a dozen hand-grenades, two Sten-guns and two pistols with several spare magazines near a window on the first floor just over the entrance door. I kept feeling a great desire to look out of the window. When I had packed as much stuff as I thought the wheels of the trailer would bear, I opened the door and loaded. I then locked up, pushed the contraption into the street, jumped on and had to stand on the pedals to make them turn. It felt like towing an elephant. I turned the corner. All was quiet. I reached the workshop and on a signal from Pierre rode right inside. The trailer was unloaded in a jiffy and I was off again. All was still quiet when I got back to the house to repeat the performance. I forget how many trips I had to make. The last visit was important—it was essential that not a scrap of evidence should be left. A single round of revolver ammunition, a small piece of the oily paper-wrapping of the H.E., a single detonator—in a word, the slightest remnant could have given the show away. I scoured all the rooms and the cellar—every recess—the cracks between the floorboards. There remained the smell—the almond odour of plastic explosive. I opened all the windows and hoped for a breeze. Then I left for the last time and reached the workshop. Georges was busy concealing the stuff in his spacious premises among the stacks of wood and the machine tools. He assured me it could never be found when he had finished. He is a jovial sort and began laughing at me. I said, 'Well, I can relax now, won't you let me in on the huge joke?'

'Why, it's you—you do look hot! I've never seen anyone sweat like that.'

He was probably right. I could feel the sweat trickling down my face and my shirt clinging to my back.

'Er, yes, of course but—well, it's a very warm day, isn't it?'

In any case nothing was found and when the police questioned the house agent the matter ended, as we had hoped, with a shrugging of shoulders.

There were so many groundless denunciations.

Liberation

I will end these reminiscences with a last memory of Paris. Honoré and I were staying with a banker at his flat in Neuilly-sur-Seine. It was there that we heard the B.B.C.'s announcement that Italy had capitulated. In order to celebrate we went up to Montmartre and had an excellent dinner in a small restaurant just off the Place du Tertre. Several artists from various cabarets came in for supper and the atmosphere became quite gay. It was truly Montmartrois as there were of course no tourists and there happened to be no Germans that evening. Some of the artists kept interrupting their meal to provide impromptu entertainment, and the rafters shook to the ribald choruses. There was a charming lady with a lovely soprano voice who sang several songs of a more conventional kind. She was in the middle of 'O Sole Mio' when the door opened and an Italian came in. Everybody burst into laughter and applauded as she finished her song. She then turned graciously to the Italian and with a sweet smile said she hoped he had not felt there had been a direct allusion to the event of the day. He grinned broadly and replied, 'Oh no, not at all—you see, from now on I am an American!' Drinks were poured out and a good time was had by all.

We felt that the war was being won—Mussolini had preceded Hitler in the path of dictatorship and swashbuckling—now he was leading the way out. The relationship between German and Italian troops on French soil would be interesting to observe in the next few days.

Honoré and I went back to the country much refreshed by our short trip to Paris.

.   .   .   .   .

From then onwards the Resistance movement, encouraged by victories and the certainty of an Allied landing, grew rapidly. Recruits multiplied, and the waverers made up their minds.

A vast literature has recorded the deeds of undercover fighters in the weeks preceding and following June 6th, 1944. For this reason I will interrupt, at the turning-point of the Italian surrender, these reminiscences of typical incidents in the life of a special agent in the dark earlier days.

My fourth mission ended in a simple way. I was liberated with the population of Melun by the American troops, so that I did not need to organize a 'pick-up' to return to England.

As to my dear friends, Alexandre, Honoré, Pierre, Octave and many others, they never came back. . . .